Community Psychology

Series Editors
Mohamed Seedat, Mohamed Seedat, Institute for Social and Health Sciences,
University of South Africa, Johannesburg, South Africa
South African Medical Research Council-University of South Africa Masculinity
and Health Research Unit, Cape Town, South Africa

Shahnaaz Suffla, Institute for Social and Health Sciences, University of South
Africa, Johannesburg, South Africa
South African Medical Research Council-University of South Africa Masculinity
and Health Research Unit, Capetown, South Africa

The Community Psychology book series is envisaged as a space to review the established assumptions and knowledge economy underlying community psychology, and encourage writings that recognize the plurality of people and the many geographical, psychological and sociological locations that they occupy. The book series will enable contributors to stimulate thought that questions that which is constructed as critical knowledges, community psychology, and the meanings of liberation and community. Contributions to the book series draw attention to the applications of community psychology in the Global South and the Global North as they relate to such issues as violence, socio-economic inequality, racism, gender, migration, dispossession, climate change, and disease outbreaks. In do so, it centers community psychology as focused on the well-being of collectives, and dealing with such focal issues as deploying psychology to support social justice, the relevance and appropriateness of its internal logic, and methods that deal with the range of psychological, social, cultural, economic, political, environmental, epistemic, and local and global influences that bear on the quality of life of individuals, communities and society. The book series concentrates thus on the following three key areas of focus: 1) decoloniality, power and epistemic justice, 2) knowledge production, contestation and community psychology, and 3) community psychology in context. The series is of vital and immediate relevance to researchers, practitioners, faculty and students from the intervention sciences, including anthropology, sociology, public health, development studies, social work and urban studies.

More information about this series at https://link.springer.com/bookseries/15965

Nick Malherbe

For an Anti-capitalist Psychology of Community

 Springer

Nick Malherbe
Institute for Social and Health Sciences
University of South Africa & South African Medical
Research Council-University of South Africa
Masculinity and Health Research Unit
Cape Town, South Africa

ISSN 2523-7241   ISSN 2523-725X   (electronic)
Community Psychology

ISBN 978-3-030-99698-7   ISBN 978-3-030-99696-3   (eBook)
https://doi.org/10.1007/978-3-030-99696-3

This Springer imprint is published by the registered company Springer Nature Switzerland AG
The registered company address is: Gewerbestrasse 11, 6330 Cham, Switzerland

Foreword

The Community Psychology Book Series: A Dialogical Decolonising Space

The Springer Community Psychology Book Series holds an ambitious vision that approaches community psychology as a site of knowledge and knowledge-making. The Series is imagined as a dialogical space for critical and situated knowledges and liberatory praxes. Through interrogations of decolonising psychologies' obligations in the era of the modern knowledge economy, and the embrace of alternative, disruptive, and new imaginings, the Book Series intends to elaborate on collective critical-liberatory projects in community psychology, and cognate areas of scholarship. The Series is however alert to the limitations imposed on creative thought and practices by hierarchical and homogenising influences in and outside of the academy.

The Series encourages contributions that focus on community psychology as knowledge, and the contestation for representation and authority. We invite contributors to examine the politics and archaeology of knowledge. Likewise, the Series draws together contributions that review how particular concepts and theories have gained ascendency in community psychology, and that offer insights into the benefits and limitations of creative methodologies applied in research, intervention, and analysis.

The Series encourages work that centrally engages with epistemicide—the deracination of other than western modes of knowing and knowledge systems—and its manifestations in scholarship on community, community-making, community resistance, and the formations of social arrangements that seek to overturn racism, racialisation, heteropatriarchy, classism, and other forms of oppressive social relations. The Series is aligned with and situated within the larger body of praxes of the South, borne out of struggles for self-determination, epistemic independence and epistemic agency, and visions and imaginations of radical humanism. The Series thus seeks to animate conversations about what it means to create and live in human formations that challenge 'race' and racism, gendered and patriarchal arrangements, inequitable economic and material arrangements, and problematic notions of sex and sexuality, as well as a range of other exclusionary-isms.

This book, *For An Anti-Capitalist Psychology of Community*, the fifth in the Series and authored by Nick Malherbe, engages with anti-capitalist political struggle as a site of struggling psychologies. Within its pages, conscious political action is never far from unconscious desire, and the fight for material justice is always also understood as the fight for dignity and psychological well-being. In its consideration of an anti-capitalist psychology of community, this book does not ignore or try to resolve the contradictory position of such a psychology. Instead, it draws on these contradictions to enliven psychology to the shifting demands—both creative and destructive—of a community-centred anti-capitalism. Using practical examples, Malherbe deals with the psychological components of building community-centred social movements that challenge neoliberal capitalism as a political system, an ideology, and a mode of governing rationality. The book also offers several theoretical contributions that grapple with how an anti-capitalist psychology of community can remain attentive to the psychological elements of anti-capitalist struggle; what the psychological can tell us about anti-capitalist politics; and how these politics can shape the psychological.

Institute for Social and Health Sciences,   Mohamed Seedat
University of South Africa, Johannesburg, South Africa   Shahnaaz Suffla
South African Medical Research Council-University
of South Africa Masculinity and Health Research Unit,
Cape Town, South Africa

Preface

For those committed to some sort of anti-capitalist politics, the discipline of psychology tends to be regarded with a mixture of dismissiveness and suspicion. And rightly so. It is no coincidence that both psychology and industrial capitalism began to accrue global hegemony together, almost at a stroke, in the early twentieth century (Parker, 2014). Psychology in the main functioned, and continues to function, as a colonising apparatus for adapting people to an inhumane political economy (Malherbe et al., 2021). Mainstream community psychology has not fared much better here. Despite intervening in the abhorrent individualism that characterises so much of psychology, most formalised community psychology remains silent on issues of class (issues that are inherently raced and gendered) and has even less to say about the existential imperative of anti-capitalism (Gokani & Walsh, 2017).

Is it not, then, pointless to try and compose a psychology, of any kind, that opposes the very capitalist economy that psychology has, historically, been used to bolster and legitimise? Would anti-capitalists not be better off abandoning psychology altogether? Although some have answered these questions in the affirmative (see Parker, 2014; Pavón-Cuéllar, 2017), I am not so convinced. In this book, I do not ignore or try to resolve the contradictory position of what I am calling (perhaps rather clumsily) an anti-capitalist psychology of community. Rather, in taking inspiration from Marx at his dialectical best (e.g. Marx, 1977), I use these contradictions to ensure that such a psychology moves with the shifting demands of anti-capitalism. Embracing contradiction in this way rejects the fixed signs and stable identifications on which much psychology is premised (Malherbe, 2021), and instead attunes psychology to the ways that it can (and should not) be used to negate and create in accordance with the democratically determined demands of anti-capitalism (see Holloway, 2010).

Perhaps, though, the basic argument for an anti-capitalist psychology of community lies in the fact that political struggle is always, at once, a site of struggling psychologies. While it is readily acknowledged that anti-capitalist activity contains political antagonisms (see Laclau & Mouffe, 1985), it is less often the case that such activity is understood as an intersubjective process characterised by anguish, elation, suffering, trust, resentment, disappointment, joy, love, regret, deceit, and a host of other psychological phenomena. Conscious political action is never far from unconscious desire, and the fight for material justice is always also the fight for dignity and psychological well-being. As such, an anti-capitalist psychology of community is attentive to the psychological elements of anti-capitalist struggle; what the psychological can tell us about anti-capitalist politics; and how these politics can bend and shape the psychological.

Although I will stress this point many times in the following chapters, it is worth mentioning here too: this book's account of an anti-capitalist psychology of community reflects my personal experiences. It is not my intention (nor, I hope, anyone else's) to approximate the definitive content of such a psychology. I have sought to hold the contradictions of this psychology in very particular ways and settings. I can only hope that others will do the same, and in so doing we can remake psychology so that it services the anti-capitalist imperative upon which the freedom of all communities depends.

Cape Town, South Africa   Nick Malherbe

References

Gokani, R., & Walsh, R. T. (2017). On the historical and conceptual foundations of a community psychology of social transformation. *American Journal of Community Psychology*, 59(3-4), 284-294.

Holloway, J. (2010). *Crack capitalism*. Pluto Press.

Laclau, E. & Mouffe, C. (1985). *Hegemony and socialist strategy: Towards a radical democratic politics*. Verso.

Malherbe, N. (2021). De-ideologization, liberation psychology, and the place of contradiction. *Journal for the Theory of Social Behaviour*. Advance online publication doi:10.1111/jtsb.12322

Malherbe, N., Ratele, K., Adams, G., Reddy, G., & Suffla, S. (2021). A decolonial Africa(n)-centered psychology of antiracism. *Review of General Psychology, 25*(4), 437-450.

Marx, K. (1977). *Capital: A critique of political economy, Vol. 1*. Vintage.

Parker, I. (2014). *Psychology after the crisis: Scientific paradigms and political debate*. Routledge.

Pavón-Cuéllar, D. (2017). *Marxism and psychoanalysis: In or against psychology?* Routledge.

Acknowledgements

It is, of course, customary for those publishing in Springer's Community Psychology book series to acknowledge the terrific support provided by Mohamed Seedat and Shahnaaz Suffla, the editors of the series. Here, I am no different. Both professors provided me with illuminating insights and expert guidance throughout the writing of this book. Their critical comments also proved fundamental to the form that the book eventually took. What immediately comes to mind are Shahnaaz's gentle challenges to my idealistic faith in the democratic process; Mohamed's reminder that decrying everything with which I disagree as "bourgeois" is not, in fact, analysis; and both professors' insistence on using decolonial theory to analyse capitalism's global purview. However, I wish to depart from the usual kinds of acknowledgements that Mohamed and Shahnaaz receive as editors, as I must also thank them for the support, lessons, opportunities, and kindness that they have shown to me as mentors over the last 8 years. It is under their tutelage that I have taken on what I would ordinarily understand to be far beyond my capabilities.

To the many residents of Thembelihle with whom I have worked over the years. Their patience, sharp criticism, humour, and hospitality have made this work pleasurable, challenging, and deeply educational. My engagements with the Thembelihle Crisis Committee, Chasing our Dreams, and Isibani have been especially rewarding.

To the two institutions within which I work, the University of South Africa's Institute for Social and Health Sciences and the South Medical Research Council-University of South Africa, Masculinity and Health Research Unit must also be acknowledged for their support. The remarkable people with whom I have worked at these institutions have all, in some way, contributed to this book.

My thanks also to Cathy, Antoine, and Meggie for their support over the years.

Conversations with several people influenced the writing of this book. My gratitude extends to Rebecca Helman, Sipho Dlamini, Sarah Day, Refiloe Makama, Neziswa Titi, Royal Lekoba, Samed Bulbulia, Graham Strickland, Elliot Kotze, Brett Martindale, Ghouwa Ismail, Maxine Rubin, Ray van Wyk, Umesh Bawa, Rashid Ahmed, Kelle Howson, Ben Gidlow, Lani Spice, Isabelle Bouic, Brittany Everitt-Penhale, Debbie Kaminer, Naiema Taliep, Kopano Ratele, Alison Stewart, Ashley van Niekerk, Alex Freeman, Ursula Lau, Daniel Radebe, Bongani Mavundla,

Lu-Anne Swart, Seneca Louw, Jade Morkel, Noxolo Dumani, Zayaan Goolam, Pascal Richardson, Abiodun Oladejo, Najuwa Arendse, Nomagugu Ngwenya, and doubtless many others.

I must make special mention of Josephine Cornell, the very best friend and colleague anyone could wish for. Many of the ideas in this book are probably Josie's. I'm just not sure which ones.

Lastly, I wish to thank Sam Lawrenson, whose loving insights, humour, unceasing kindness, and wisdom mean the whole world to me.

Contents

Chapter 1
How Should We Understand an Anti-Capitalist Psychology of Community?

Although critical psychology—broadly conceived—can be of use to anti-capitalist struggle, it has, for the most part, been of relatively little use (Collins, 2003). Anti-capitalism is certainly not novel within psychology, but it remains rather marginal, with considerations of political economy and social class rarely foregrounded in an explicit manner by psychologists (Gokani & Walsh, 2017; Malherbe, 2018, 2021; Parker, 2015; Zlotowitz & Burton, 2022). Nonetheless, there are some critical psychologists who have made anti-capitalism central to their work. As such, before I define what it is I mean by an anti-capitalist psychology of community, I wish to make it clear that I am not laying claim to having invented such a psychology. Moreover, I am not attempting in this book to chronicle the different ways that a psychology of community has, historically, embraced anti-capitalism (for some excellent accounts here, see Burton & Guzzo, 2020; Fryer, 2008; Hollander, 1997; Gaztambide, 2019; Montero et al., 2017; Seedat & Lazarus, 2011). Instead, the goals of this book are rather different. Firstly, I draw on my experience as a community psychologist working in South Africa to demonstrate how—at a theoretical and at a practical level—anti-capitalism (i.e. opposition to the kinds of ownership, economic relations, and distributive practices that characterise a capitalist political economy; see Tormey, 2004) can inform a psychology of community (i.e. an embrace of the liberation psychology paradigm from within the tradition of critical community psychology; see Montero et al., 2017). Secondly, I explore what it is that a psychology of community can offer to anti-capitalist struggle. In so doing, I emphasise that a psychology of community should not capitulate to the psychologisation of anti-capitalism (e.g. rendering anti-capitalist action the product of psychological maladjustment, rather than a reasonable response to a dehumanising social order; see Fanon, 1963; Malherbe & Ratele, 2022; Pavón-Cuéllar, 2017) and that psychological theories and practices must bend in accordance with the political requirements of anti-capitalism. The book, in short, explores some of the ways that a psychology of community can serve those anti-capitalist movements and moments that seek to reconstitute the material world in more equitable ways. The book's title thus confers a double meaning: it is a book that is to be used *for* the development of an anti-capitalist psychology of community (building on theories, practices, tactics, methods, and strategies), while, at the same time, it advocates *for* the existence of such a psychology, loosely formalising it without fully institutionalising it.

In this introductory chapter, I posit that it makes little less sense to offer definitive explanations of an anti-capitalist psychology of community. The reason for this is that anti-capitalism and a psychology of community, quite simply, do not weld together in an easy union. Neither is a homogenous concept (there are many approaches to anti-capitalism just as there are several psychologies of community), and the core elements of each do not always permit synthesis (e.g. the global purview of anti-capitalism does not necessarily complement the localised focus of a psychology of community). Yet, this inability of an anti-capitalist psychology of community to cohere with itself is, I will argue, to its advantage. The contradictions that mark this kind of psychology render it a psychology of movement, adaptability, and development—a psychology of becoming rather than of being. As we shall see, by embracing—instead of papering over—its internal contradictions, a psychology of community can ground itself in the shifting contextual requirements of anti-capitalism, many of which will undoubtedly contrast with the disciplinary demands of institutionalised psychology (Malherbe, 2021).

In what follows, I try to capture the dialectical nature of an anti-capitalist psychology of community and thus forgo any attempt to delineate its precise content. After defining anti-capitalism and a psychology of community, I offer an understanding of an anti-capitalist psychology of community that embraces its inherent contradictions and what it means to hold, instead of overcome, these contradictions (see Malherbe, 2018; McGowan, 2019; Parker, 2015). I then conclude by outlining the structure of this book and in so doing reflect on some of its shortcomings and potentialities.

What Is Anti-Capitalism?

Wherever there has been capitalism, there has, historically, also been anti-capitalism (Wright, 2019). Although a broad term, anti-capitalism describes the political disposition of those who stand in opposition to the limiting kinds of ownership, socioeconomic relations, and distributive avenues that are available under capitalism (Tormey, 2004). There is, however, a problem of negativity in this definition of anti-capitalism. How can we build a politics of any kind through an orientation that is characterised by what it is in opposition to? If we are *anti*-capitalist, what exactly are we *for*? Might anti-capitalism not lead to something even more exploitative than capitalism, like fascism? While these conceptual critiques of anti-capitalism are certainly valid, I am with Robert Latham (2018), who argues that the most effective, sustainable iterations of anti-capitalism have always been formally diverse and politically left-wing. It is when anti-capitalism is leftist and diverse that it can harness the negation of *anti* as a creative force, whereby a new, non-capitalist society is not predetermined, but is built through collective democratic will. In other words, we need not embrace *anti* as a deficit, but as a reflective and generative point that opens us up to a variety of anti-capitalisms. Contrary to many contemporary characterisations of his work, Karl Marx championed a creative and multitudinous anti-capitalism of this sort. Anti-capitalist socialists, he wrote, should not concern themselves with "writing recipes for the cookshops of the future" (Marx, 1977, p. 99). Instead, Marx advocated for a post-capitalist society (which he spoke of as communism) premised on the relatively non-prescriptive dictum: from each according to ability to each according to need (Marx, 1978a). We should not, therefore, understand anti-capitalism as a prefigured political programme that prohibits people from altering their viewpoints. It is a political posture (see Harvey, 2020) that is subject to democratically led change and, when assumed, can be used to create solidarity within complex, fragmented class structures (see Wright, 2019). At the same time, anti-capitalism does not approach *anti* as an endpoint: a constant state of resistance devoid of any political programme. As John Holloway (2010) insists, anti-capitalism is not merely refusal; there is always "another-doing implicit in the No" (p. 29). Anti-capitalism, in essence then, relies on *anti* to emphasise the many different paths that we can take to build an intersectional socialism wherein harmony between people and the land on which they live is advanced through the democratic control of surplus value, production, as well as the cultural, natural, and social commonwealth.

Anti-capitalism has always been multitudinous. By the end of the nineteenth century, it assumed many, often disparate, formations (Tormey, 2004). Today, as people like David Harvey (2020) remind us, we can see anti-capitalism at the point of production (e.g. strikes), realisation in the market (e.g. boycotts), and social reproduction (e.g. struggles for food security). We also see anti-capitalism in the so-called boundary struggles over ecology, land seizures, dispossession, and political power (Fraser, 2014). Moreover, anti-capitalism is observed throughout the Global South whenever attempts are made to de-link local economies from the globalised capitalist economy (Amin, 1990). While today's anti-capitalisms have, at times, been promoted by political parties, they are perhaps more often the products of environmental movements, indigenous movements, labour struggles, direct action initiatives, grassroots community organising, anti-globalisation struggles, and even some non-governmental organisations (Tormey, 2004). Although anti-capitalisms have, historically, been uneven in their effectiveness (Latham, 2018), they tend to be at their strongest when they are forged through coalitions with one another. This is why anti-capitalists stress the importance of solidarity (see Featherstone, 2012).

There are, however, anti-capitalisms that are neither diverse nor left-wing. Indeed, there are liberal and even right-wing political discourses that draw on anti-capitalist rhetoric (Harvey, 2020). Yet, discourses of this sort tend to advocate for the continuation of capitalism by other means, such as fascism (Yeros & Jha, 2020), and in this sense draw on the persuasiveness of anti-capitalism to advance capitalist ends. Anti-capitalism is also not immune to its politics being gradually blunted from within as well as from without. In what Guy Debord (1977) and the Situationist International called "ideological recuperation" (see also Parker, 2009), anti-capitalist tactics can become subsumed by capitalist logic (e.g. through so-called ethical consumption) or by what Mark Fisher (2009) called capitalist realism, where capitalist rationality is so totalising that even our visions of anti-capitalism fail to imagine a world outside of capitalist logic. Those looking to build a left-wing, diverse anti-capitalism must, therefore, remain attuned to the political ends to which anti-capitalist struggle is directed and must guard against anti-capitalism being used as a mere rhetorical flourish.

How can we make sense of diverse anti-capitalist struggles and the ways that they operate alongside, independent from, and with one another? In *How to Be an Anticapitalist in the Twenty-First Century*, the last book he published in his lifetime, Erik Olin Wright (2019) provides a helpful taxonomy wherein he delineates five kinds of anti-capitalist strategy. The first of these strategies he calls smashing capitalism, which refers to the revolutionary overthrow of the capitalist system. We saw several attempts at smashing capitalism in the twentieth century, oftentimes in the Global South. Successfully smashing capitalism is, however, increasingly unlikely today. As Harvey (2020) has argued (somewhat controversially, I should add; see Martín, 2020), contemporary capitalism is, in many ways, too big to fail. He insists that all over the world, the delivery of food, fuel, and energy—as well as sustaining everyday life and globalised communication networks—depends on the circulation of capital and commodities. Smashing capitalism is, thus, not only unlikely, but it would have detrimental effects that would be exacerbated in the Global South (see Amin, 2010). Today's anti-capitalist politics would do well to keep in mind that a peaceful transition from capitalism is less often a singular event than it is an organised and sustained process (Harvey, 2020). It is perhaps for these reasons that Wright (2019) takes more seriously the following four anti-capitalist strategies which, when applied together, are able to *erode* capitalism.

Dismantling capitalism, the first of Wright's (2019) erosive anti-capitalist strategies, occurs through electoral politics. Although there are, today, fewer anti-capitalist political parties than ever before, anti-capitalism is not entirely absent in the electoral arena. In Bolivia, Peru, Chile, and—albeit to a lesser extent—New Zealand, for example, the governing political parties were all democratically elected on explicitly anti-capitalist campaigns. The next erosive anti-capitalist strategy that Wright (2019) outlines is known as taming capitalism, which speaks to reformist and regulatory measures (see also Tormey, 2004). The choice for those looking to tame capitalism is not a false one between reform and revolution. Rather, to tame capitalism is to enact a protracted revolution through progressive reform that sets the stage for more structurally oriented changes (see Harvey, 2009). Reforms of this sort do not seek to find a way out of the crises of capitalism. They move us towards abandoning a capitalism that has always been in crisis (Amin, 2010). Wright's (2019) third erosive anti-capitalist strategy, resisting capitalism, infers political struggles which take place outside of the State and that do not attempt to gain State power. Latham (2018) writes that resisting capitalism can take the form of cessation, wherein a particular facet of capitalism is targeted (e.g. austerity), or deflection, which refers to pulling away from capitalism altogether (e.g. a strike). Wright's (2019) final erosive anti-capitalist strategy is what he calls escaping capitalism, whereby micro-alternatives to capitalism are created within capitalist political economies. Wright (2019) refers to these micro-alternatives as "real utopias" which institute, in the present, aspects of a desired future wherein people's political goals structure and organise the ways by which they live in the present (see Featherstone, 2012). Considered together, Wright's (2019) four erosive anti-capitalist strategies imply that there are both moral and practical components to anti-capitalism, with the former used to assess the latter and the latter drawn on to realise the former.

We should not underplay the difficulties of actioning anti-capitalist strategy. Anti-capitalist activity takes a physical as well as a psychological toll. Moreover, because for most people life under capitalism is precarious, they are ensnared in the "inertia of survival" (Žižek, 2018 p. 69), whereby their energies are devoted to sustaining their basic existence. When one is living just to survive, politics can seem superfluous, which makes gaining support for anti-capitalist activities rather challenging. Anti-capitalism is also not, in every instance, devoid of abuse between supposed comrades. Many female and transgender comrades, for instance, continue to experience patriarchal attitudes and outright violence within anti-capitalist movements, just as many Black comrades have been subjected to racist treatment within these movements (Wilkinson, 2017). Marx, himself, exhibited many racist and sexist positions that were typical of the White, Victorian patriarchal attitudes that informed much European anti-capitalism in the nineteenth century (see Eagleton, 2011; Malherbe, 2018). It is, therefore, crucial that if anti-capitalism is to accrue the kind of broad-based appeal that it needs to survive, it must be made into an attractive and commonsensical imperative. This means that it must address the totality of capitalism, including its imperial, patriarchal, and racist guises (Amin, 2010, 2014). An anti-capitalism of this sort is concerned not only with taking power but with taking power differently so that oppressive action no longer receives structural support (Hardt & Negri, 2017).

If we approach capitalism as a form of structural violence (see Galtung, 1969, and Chap. 2), then anti-capitalism can be understood as a kind of counter-violence that addresses itself not only to capitalism's violent, dehumanising value system, but also to how the oppression of labour in the Global North relies on the murderous hyper-exploitation of workers in the Global South (Amin, 2010). Conceiving of anti-capitalism as counter-violence is, however, not without complications. Although many successful anti-capitalist campaigns have, throughout history, taken place with very little bloodshed (Eagleton, 2011), thinkers like Frantz Fanon (1963) have argued that the most effective kinds of anti-capitalism will always be represented as violent by capitalist colonial powers who are anxious to hold onto their monopoly on violence. The violence that may accompany anti-capitalism can, therefore, be seen as an attempt to redirect the violence of capitalist domination, striking back at those dominating power structures which produce violence, daily, in the lives of most people (Hardt & Negri, 2009). Although some equate anti-capitalism with violence, for others, violence may be deployed to defend anti-capitalism. Walter Benjamin (2007) speaks of anti-capitalism as representing a kind of "divine violence" that rejects capitalism's ruinously hierarchical imposition (which he calls "mythic violence"). It is through divine violence that anti-capitalism offers instances of nonviolence that can be seized upon and systemised. For Judith Butler (2020), though, it is because violence cannot be contained or distilled into a manageable form that anti-capitalism must strive towards nonviolence, which she argues is not a passive or inert disposition, but a force that solidifies equitable social bonds between comrades and the society in and upon which they act. In considering all of this, we might conclude that although anti-capitalism aspires towards a society that negates the kinds of violence inherent to capitalism, we should retain a critical understanding of how violence is used and misused in characterisations and enactments of anti-capitalism.

Before moving to the next section on a psychology of community, I wish to concede that, for me, there is no greater theorist of capitalism than Marx, and thus it is to the Marxist tradition that I owe much of my understanding of anti-capitalism. To deny the profound influence that Marxist theory has had on this book would be disingenuous. That being said, I am well aware of the limitations of Marxism. Marx was not always right or consistent, and he was oftentimes myopic in his anti-capitalist politics (Malherbe, 2018). However, he was right enough of the time, in my view, that his analyses serve as indispensable for advancing anti-capitalist struggles in our time (see also Amin, 2010; Eagleton, 2011). Yet, as Hardt and Negri (2004) posit, because Marx's historical materialist method requires that we shape anti-capitalist theory in accordance with social reality, working in the tradition of Marxism often means that we must step away from Marx and go beyond his proposals. A truly "creative Marxism" impels us "not to stop at Marx, but to start from him" and to subject Marxism itself to anti-capitalist critique (Amin, 2010, p. 9–10). I am, therefore, with Fanon (1963) who called on us not to do away with Marx's interventions entirely, but to stretch Marxism so that it accommodates an expansive vision of anti-capitalism, one that is attendant to and forges alliances with class struggles that are not, in every instance, obviously proletarian (e.g. feminist, antiracist, indigenous, decolonial, and ecological struggles). Although Marx may not have been especially concerned with these kinds of struggles, they have always preoccupied those working in and against the most critical variants of the Marxist tradition. Perhaps it is best to give the last word on this book's relationship with Marxism to Stuart Hall, who saw his own project as "working within shouting distance of Marxism, working on Marxism, working against Marxism, working with it, working to try to develop Marxism" (Hall, 1992, p. 279).

What Is a Psychology of Community?

A psychology of community, as I define it, refers to the tradition of critical community psychology that has embraced the liberation psychology paradigm (see Montero et al., 2017, for a comprehensive discussion here). In this section, I discuss a psychology of community over three stages: first, I define what is meant by critical community psychology; second, I outline some of the key features of liberation psychology; and third, I offer some reflections on how critical community psychology can and has embraced the liberation psychology paradigm, forming what I am calling a psychology of community.

All over the world, critical community psychology emerged in the 1970s as a reaction to what was understood as the conservative and politically regressive currents within mainstream community psychology (Montero, 1996). Some have, however, argued that critical ways of practising psychology within communities existed long before the 1970s (e.g. Fryer, 2008), meaning that we should perhaps understand critical community psychology as encompassing multiple histories (Stevens, 2007). Although critical community psychology represents a range of politically progressive approaches to community psychology, it always takes social justice as its point of departure and in this way constitutes an ever-evolving approach to psychosocial wellbeing, rather than a rigid set of disciplinary orthodoxies (Evans et al., 2017). As such, critical community psychology tends to align with the political agendas of social movements which are concerned with addressing the structural nature of oppression (Burton & Kagan, 2015; Fryer, 2008). Action, social change, and political commitment (rather than theory, permissiveness, and neutrality) are thereby central to critical community psychology praxes (Davidson et al., 2006), as is the fostering of critical consciousness, which Paulo Freire (1972) conceptualised as an attempt to understand oppressive social conditions so that we might change these conditions at a structural level. Relatedly, power—especially social and political power—is a pertinent concern for critical community psychology (Watts & Serrano-García, 2003). As Sandy Lazarus (2018) asserts, critical community psychologists work "alongside those most harmed, exposing the psycho-social and political systems that do the most harm and engaging in research and social action to support social justice" (p. 13). Those practising critical community psychology are also encouraged to address issues of power among themselves. Psychologists, community members, and social movements are, in these ways, held accountable to one another as well as to the ideals of social justice (Burton & Kagan, 2015).

In the 1970s, liberation psychology was developed as a reaction to the crisis of relevance within social psychology (Burton & Guzzo, 2020). However, the disparate histories of critical community psychology contrast somewhat with liberation psychology's trajectory, which most agree finds its formalised origins in the work of Ignacio Martín-Baró (1994), a Spanish-born social psychologist and Jesuit priest working in El Salvador. Liberation psychology has been defined as an emancipatory paradigm or process from which to undertake psychology (Malherbe, 2018), whereby liberation is, itself, conceived of as that which can only be pursued by oppressed majorities, rather than handed over by a privileged elite (Montero et al., 2017). Psychologists who situate themselves in this paradigm work in solidarity with poor and marginalised peoples to understand how oppression is maintained through political, economic, cultural, and social systems and institutions (Enriquez, 1992; Martín-Baró, 1994). In this, the structural roots of oppression are identified in an attempt to understand, and ultimately alleviate, psychic and material distress. Although these aims are similar to those of critical community psychology, liberation psychology tends to be more politically radical in its approach (see Reich et al., 2017). Martín-Baró (1994), perhaps in an attempt to distinguish his work from community psychology, argued that liberation psychology constitutes three elements: (1) a new horizon, whereby psychology is to concern itself with the needs of majority populations rather than institutional legitimacy; (2) a new epistemology, where psychological knowledges are conceived of as democratically constructed, rather than singularly discovered; and (3) a new praxis, where people combine theory and practice to collectively catalyse socially transformative change. These three elements have been advanced in several ways, including participatory action research, qualitative and quantitative research, de-ideologisation, de-alienation, the recovery of historical memory, fostering critical consciousness, problematisation, and de-naturalisation (see Malherbe, 2018; Martín-Baró, 1994; Montero et al., 2017). In recent years, there has been a resurgence of liberation psychology praxes that have taken up the decolonial attitude in important ways, especially in the Global South (see, e.g. Boonzaier & van Niekerk, 2019; Carolissen & Duckett, 2018; Kessi et al., 2022; Seedat & Suffla, 2017b; Stevens & Sonn, 2021). In sum, liberation psychology represents an action-oriented and a contextually sensitive way of working with oppressed people to analyse and improve their psycho-social-material realities (Malherbe, 2018; Montero & Sonn, 2009) and to approach mental health not as a set of "natural facts" (Fisher, 2009, p. 19), but as psychological processes that are lodged within a society's political economy. As such, psychological problems are addressed with collective modes of political action that are attuned to issues of identity, knowledge, consciousness, and culture (Enriquez, 1992; Watkins & Shulman, 2008).

It has been said that critical community psychology has taken to the liberation psychology paradigm more than any other field of psychology (Montero & Sonn, 2009). Certainly, the similarities between the two (e.g. a focus on power, culture, participation, consciousness-raising, praxis, affect, justice, community engagement, and structural oppression) have meant that the distinctive boundaries between each are not always clearly demarcated (Montero et al., 2017). What, we might ask, is the point of collapsing liberation psychology and critical community psychology under a single signifier (namely, a psychology of community) if both are so similar and even, in some cases, difficult to distinguish from one another? I maintain that there are ontological and epistemological differences between the two and when we hold both together, each can embolden the other in different ways. For instance, the embeddedness of most critical community psychologists within institutions, no matter how critical they may be of these institutions, can make available the resources required to realise the emancipatory ideals of liberation psychology, which is often under-resourced. In turn, liberation psychology can offer critical community psychologists lessons in resisting and imaginatively circumventing constraining institutional demands (see Reich et al., 2017) all while ensuring that critical community psychologists avoid unwittingly psychologising social movements through pseudo-progressive language (Gokani & Walsh, 2017; Malherbe & Dlamini, 2020). Liberation psychology can offer critical community psychology several important concepts (e.g. de-alienation, de-ideologisation, and problematisation) which can be harnessed in novel ways to advance the goals of critical community psychology (e.g. consciousness-raising, interdisciplinarity, and collective action). Similarly, global developments within critical community psychology may be useful for reinterpreting those concerns within liberation psychology (e.g. fatalist ideology) which take their epistemological bearings from particular 1970s' Latin American contexts (see Montero et al., 2017; Reich et al., 2017). Liberation psychology's embrace of psychoanalysis (see Hollander, 1997; Malherbe, 2021) can also assist critical community psychologists to interrogate the unconscious elements which comprise a psychological sense of community (see Sarason, 1974). In short, embracing the liberation psychology paradigm from within the tradition of critical community psychology to form what I am calling a psychology of community can allow for ambitious, multifarious approaches to enacting psychosocial justice.

Epistemologically, a psychology of community draws on community psychology and liberation psychology to engage the subject-in-context in very particular ways. Indeed, psychological subjects are understood as always psychosocial subjects who are continually reformed by communities and one another, exercising agency and remaking their subjectivity in and against the limits of the social and institutional structures within which they are embedded (Martín-Baró, 1994; Malherbe & Ratele, 2022; Seedat & Suffla, 2017a). Similarly, a community is not perceived as a static geographic space that is to be either valorised or demonised (Malherbe et al., 2021). Instead, community represents an inconsistent process that constitutes shifting modes of connection and exclusion which can be remade for political purposes, including social justice, collective dignity, and equality. In this regard, a psychology of community challenges how community psychologists understand both psychology and community.

For me, the essence of a psychology of community can be found in attempts to practise psychology in a politically progressive manner. Such a psychology gives to psychologists and those with whom they work a means by which to enact, or attempt to enact, a form of psychosocial praxis that extends beyond psychology's disciplinary and institutional boundaries and that does not compromise collective visions of emancipation. It is in this regard that a psychology of community attends to the dynamic visions, politics, goals, and demands of those engaged in collective struggle (see Malherbe & Ratele, 2022).

Grasping at an Anti-Capitalist Psychology of Community through Contradiction

Some argue that psychology has nothing to offer anti-capitalist struggle, evidenced most clearly by the discipline's history of interpreting anti-capitalism as a kind of psychopathology (see Pavón-Cuéllar, 2017). At best, the argument goes, psychologists involved in anti-capitalist activity can evoke their discipline as an unnecessary sort of indulgence (Drury, 2003; Parker, 2009). Others, however, have insisted that anti-capitalism and psychology can inform one another, with the former stretching the latter beyond itself (see Pavón-Cuéllar et al., 2015). Indeed, for my own purposes, we can look to several instances where anti-capitalism has been incorporated into a psychology of community (e.g. Arfken, 2011; de Oliveira & Júnior, 2022; Hamber et al., 2001; *Melancholic Troglodytes*, 2003; Pavón-Cuéllar et al., 2015; Seedat & Lazarus, 2011; Zlotowitz & Burton, 2022). I, myself, have argued that a psychology of community can—if it is to be effective—assume an anti-capitalist posture in how it approaches mental distress, competitive individualisation, and the debilitating desires that are fostered by a capitalist political economy (Malherbe, 2018, 2021).

In this section, I argue that an anti-capitalist psychology of community, if it is to be understood as moving and shifting in accordance with the anti-capitalist demands of the moment, cannot be formulated through fixed points of commonality that exist between anti-capitalism and a psychology of community. Instead, I claim, by defining an anti-capitalist psychology of community by its internal contradictions (i.e. the ways that this kind of psychology is not quite at one with itself; see McGowan, 2019), we are afforded a generative means of understanding its capacities and utility (imagined and existing) all while ensuring that the content of such a psychology is open to democratic negotiation as well as the psychological and material requirements of anti-capitalism (Malherbe, 2021). Contradiction, in other words, can assist us in ensuring that an anti-capitalist psychology of community is determined by the dynamism of social change initiatives and not the other way around (Malherbe & Dlamini, 2020; Malherbe & Ratele, 2022). When we define an anti-capitalist psychology of community by its contradictions, we seek to ensure that it does not assume a given or settled form. It is, instead, a psychology that is provoked, reflected upon, and realised in anti-capitalist action (Pavón-Cuéllar, 2017). Under the signifier *anti-capitalist psychology of community*, we can hold the contradictions of psychology, community, and anti-capitalism together in dialectical tension, rather than seek out a perfect synthesis between them, and as such, we can re-interpret each of these concepts through the registers of the others (see Parker, 2015).

One of the central contradictions of an anti-capitalist psychology of community concerns the change-making capacities of the political subject. In many conceptions of anti-capitalism (I am thinking here of its orthodox Marxian variants), it is the proletarian class—due to its embeddedness in capitalism's "nerve centre" of production—that can institute the most effective sort of anti-capitalist resistance (Malherbe, 2018). For a psychology of community, however, all subaltern and marginalised social groups (and perhaps also those belonging to more privileged groups who are willing to abandon their positions within the social hierarchy) are understood as effective change-making agents (Seedat & Suffla, 2017a). Under the banner of anti-capitalism, change-making processes range considerably in their relationship to violence (where some reject the category of violence altogether, others trouble how we understand violence, while others claim that capitalist violence can only be countered with anti-capitalist violence), whereas a psychology of community tends to be much less ambiguous here, rejecting violence altogether. Another contradiction that marks an anti-capitalist psychology of community is related to scope. Although anti-capitalism tends to begin from the local, its compulsion towards solidarity as well as challenging a globalised imperialist capitalist system renders it internationalist in its purview (Amin, 1990, 2014; Harvey, 2020). This jars somewhat with a psychology of community, which is usually grounded in a very particular community context (Burton & Kagan, 2009). The role of the State presents another contradiction for an anti-capitalist psychology of community. From the socialist welfare State, to the anarchist abolition of the State, to a Marxian "withering away" of the State, anti-capitalism presents a range of fierce debates and theoretical engagements with regard to the role of the State in the emancipatory process. A psychology of community has, however, remained somewhat ambiguous with respect to the role of the State in processes of psychosocial liberation (see Malherbe, 2018), sometimes working with it and other times against it (especially with respect to public policy) but rarely speaking of its relationship with the State in an explicit manner (for some exceptions here, see Javorka, 2021; Van Niekerk et al., 2014; Zlotowitz & Burton, 2022). Similarly, where anti-capitalism is, by its very nature, opposed to neoliberal institutions, a psychology of community, if it is not already embedded within these institutions, often operates alongside them, relying on them for funding, resources, and legitimacy (see Reich et al., 2017). As such, we find contradictions in how the practice of an anti-capitalist psychology of community differs from some of its theoretical ideals.

Each of the above contradictions, as well as the many others that mark an anti-capitalist psychology of community, points towards the internal instability of this kind of psychology. I have, therefore, not provided a stable point of identification for those wishing to practise such a psychology. However, as noted earlier, this is advantageous. Through these contradictions, psychologists of community can attune their work to the anti-capitalist requirements of the moment (see Malherbe, 2021), moving with what this moment demands in terms of emancipatory negation and creation (Holloway, 2010). We can, for instance, draw on the resources of an institutionalised psychology of community while, at the same time, push back against the forms of neoliberalisation that come with such proximity to capitalist institutions (e.g. strategically diverting a portion of research funding to anti-capitalist organising in the way that Martín-Baró did; see Martín-Baró, 1994). Moreover, by holding these contradictions with one another, rather than seeking to resolve them, we can bolster enactments of an anti-capitalist psychology of community through the respective concerns of anti-capitalism and a psychology of community (e.g. ensuring that anti-capitalist organising is conducted in a psychologically sensitive manner while retaining a materialist bent within community-oriented psychological work). Being attuned to these contradictions pushes psychologists to seek out not only resistance but also liberation in everyday life, organised politics, subjectivity, affective states, and social relations.

Some will certainly object to my formulation of an anti-capitalist psychology of community, claiming that if we enact psychology—any psychology—through its contradictions (i.e. dialectically), then we can no longer be said to be practising psychology (see Pavón-Cuéllar, 2017). However, perhaps we can understand an anti-capitalist psychology of community as a different kind of psychology, an anti-psychological psychology that is not concerned with preserving the psy-disciplines as we know them (see Malherbe & Ratele, 2022). When we embrace, rather than ignore or try to neatly resolve, the different ways by which an anti-capitalist psychology of community does not quite cohere with itself, we open up space for legitimising and building a plethora of anti-capitalist values, visions, practices, institutions, tactics, social arrangements, lifestyles, political activities, and hopes. If, indeed, we approach anti-capitalism as impure and premised on the dictum: "there is no Right Answer, just millions of experiments" (Holloway, 2010, p. 256), then an anti-capitalist psychology of community should strive to make itself of use to these experiments. I am, therefore, insisting that it is through contradiction that an anti-capitalist psychology of community remains alive to the movement of possibilities, both grand and humble, of living and achieving a life beyond the crippling limitations of the capitalist imaginary.

Structure of this Book

There are books that are critical of capitalism which devote much, if not all, of their attention to understanding the oppressive nature of capitalism. These books tend to conclude with a perfunctory, sometimes superfluous, note of anti-capitalist aspiration. As evidenced in this chapter, I have found many of these books very useful. However, there is also the danger that these books engender hopelessness and resignation, implying that although things can change, it is unlikely that they ever will. Added to this, many of these books exemplify the cautious distance that most academics, even those who ascribe to anti-capitalist values, tend to keep from existing anti-capitalist struggle. Therefore, in heeding Marx's (1978b) insistence that analysing capitalism is useful only insofar as it informs anti-capitalist action, I have reversed the formula of so many anti-capitalist books, dedicating just one chapter to understanding capitalism and the rest to anti-capitalist resistance. Moreover, in an attempt to break from the so-called theory industry that plagues academia, each chapter on anti-capitalist resistance concludes with a reflection on a community-based project that sought to put into practice the more abstract ideas that I discuss.

This book is personal in that it reflects my own interests, experiences, and biases. It is because I have more experience with resisting and escaping capitalism than I have had with taming and dismantling capitalism that the former two anti-capitalist strategies receive the lion's share of attention in this book. Those sites of anti-capitalism—such as pedagogy, electoral politics, ecological struggle, militancy in the workplace, and top-down resistance—with which I have had little experience rarely feature in this book. Moreover, my training has been in community psychology rather than a discipline more readily associated with anti-capitalism, like economics, sociology, history, or philosophy. Although I believe that this training has provided me with particular insights into anti-capitalism, it must also be conceded that psychology's close alignment with the capitalist project is likely to have hindered my understanding of anti-capitalism. Added to this, my background in psychology has meant that the book is perhaps more receptive to some anti-capitalisms (e.g. Marx's early humanist writings on alienation) than it is to others (e.g. Marx's later structural-historical analyses of economic exploitation). In light of all of this, there are several omissions in this book. These omissions are not unimportant to an anti-capitalist psychology of community. To the contrary, they are all the more important for others to take up.

Although each of this book's chapters focuses on a particular topic, I have tried to approach these topics as ambitiously as possible. It is unlikely that every reader will resonate with everything I cover, but I hope that some will find some of what I have to say useful. In the chapter following this one, Chap. 2, I delineate the object of the book's critique, namely, the contemporary mode of capitalism known as neoliberal capitalism, or neoliberalism. In reiterating a point made by Wendy Brown (2015), I argue that neoliberalism is a loose (but not an empty) signifier, meaning that there are several approaches we can take when trying to understand it. The three approaches that I concentrate on are neoliberalism as a political project, an ideology, and a mode of normative rationality. I then speak about how each approach relates to the other and argue that an expansive, audacious anti-capitalism must consider all three (see Amin, 2014). However, despite the fact that we cannot separate out any of these approaches from the others, I posit that one approach will always take precedence in anti-capitalist work. Indeed, because such work will, regrettably, be unable to take on the totality of capitalism, it is useful to enter into anti-capitalism through either politics, ideology, or normative rationality and from here seek to connect with and address other formations of anti-capitalist resistance. It is for these reasons that dividing capitalism (and, in the following chapters, anti-capitalist resistance) into politics, ideology, and normative rationality is both artificial and necessary. Chap. 2 ends with a consideration of how capitalism, conceived of in these three ways, has shaped mainstream conceptions of community psychology.

In the third chapter, I am concerned with how an anti-capitalist psychology of community can be of use to those who resist the neoliberal political project. Thus, I aim to outline how a psychology of community is able to work for community-based anti-capitalist resistance movements (i.e. formalised anti-capitalist collectives). The central argument of this chapter is that a psychology of community must submit to the demands of anti-capitalist community struggles. At the same time, psychologists can work with activists to challenge potential and regressive elements within their movements. Accordingly, I focus on four modes of collective anti-capitalist resistance, namely, political organising, affective community-building, solidarity-making, and reflexive engagement. I conclude by illustrating this chapter's concerns with an example from my own community-engaged work, specifically, a participatory filmmaking project that was conducted with activists and other community members from a low-income community in South Africa.

The fourth chapter speaks to how an anti-capitalist psychology of community can address neoliberal ideology. Here, I am preoccupied with how psychologists of community can work with community members to re-symbolise subjectivity, art and the popular aesthetic, and cultural memory. I insist that none of these areas in and of themselves can offer a totalising vision of anti-capitalist ideological resistance. However, together, they can afford us insights into how psychologists of community can make themselves of use to the task of creating new ideological formations that reject capitalism's oppressive social logic. In concluding this chapter, I examine how those involved in the participatory filmmaking project discussed in Chap. 3 used their film for purposes of re-symbolisation.

In the fifth chapter, I consider what psychologists of community can offer to community struggles that oppose a capitalist rationality that economises and marketises almost all aspects of our lives, including conceptions of the human. The point, here, is to make commonsensical anti-capitalist visions of the social and the individual. To do so, I consider how an anti-capitalist psychology of community can assist those who are engaged in articulating counter-hegemonic discourse, reconstituting the everyday, fighting for epistemic freedom, and fostering love and care. I then examine the anti-capitalist rationalities which were constructed by those involved in the participatory filmmaking project discussed in the previous two chapters.

In Chap. 6, the book's concluding chapter, I discuss how hope can offer those involved in an anti-capitalist psychology of community a realistic and non-deterministic confrontation with the present. Although hope does not ensure the victory of anti-capitalist struggle, without hope, there would be no anti-capitalist struggle, which makes hope a central concern of an anti-capitalist psychology of community. I consider what hope means for taking back our future from capitalism, building a more equal world, and rejecting the forces that seek to make societies and individuals in the image of infinite accumulation.

References

Amin, S. (1990). *Delinking: Towards a polycentric world*. Zed Books.
Amin, S. (2010). *The law of worldwide value*. Monthly Review Press.
Amin, S. (2014). *The implosion of capitalism*. Pluto Press.
Arfken, M. (2011). Marxism & psychology [special issue]. *Annual Review of Critical Psychology, 9*.
Benjamin, W. (2007). *Illuminations: Essays and reflections*. Schocken Books.
Boonzaier, F., & van Niekerk, T. (Eds.). (2019). *Decolonial feminist community psychology*. Springer.
Brown, W. (2015). *Undoing the demos: Neoliberalism's stealth revolution*. Zone Books.

Burton, M., & Guzzo, R. (2020). Liberation psychology: Origins and development. In L. Comas-Díaz & E. T. Rivera (Eds.), *Liberation psychology: Theory, method, practice, and social justice* (pp. 17–40). American Psychological Association.

Burton, M., & Kagan, C. (2009). Towards a really social psychology: Liberation psychology beyond Latin America. In M. Montero & C. C. Sonn (Eds.), *Psychology of liberation* (pp. 51–72). Springer.

Burton, M. H., & Kagan, C. (2015). Theory and practice for a critical community psychology in the UK. *Psicología, Conocimiento y Sociedad, 5*(2), 182–205.

Butler, J. (2020). *The force of nonviolence: The ethical in the political.* Verso.

Carolissen, R., & Duckett, P. (2018). Teaching toward decoloniality in community psychology and allied disciplines [special issue]. *American Journal of Community Psychology, 62*(3–4).

Collins, C. (2003). 'Critical psychology' and contemporary struggles against neoliberalism. *Annual Review of Critical Psychology, 3*, 26–48.

Davidson, H., Evans, S., Ganote, C., Henrickson, J., Jacobs-Priebe, L., Jones, D. L., … Riemer, M. (2006). Power and action in critical theory across disciplines: Implications for critical community psychology. *American Journal of Community Psychology, 38*(1–2), 35–49.

de Oliveira, I. F., & Júnior, F. L. (2022). Contributions of Marxism to community psychology: Emancipation in debate. In C. Kagan, J. Akhurst, J. Alfaro, R. Lawthom, M. Richards, & A. Zambrano (Eds.), *The Routledge international handbook of community psychology: Facing global crises with hope* (pp. 32–45). Routledge.

Debord, G. (1977). *Society of the spectacle.* Black & Red.

Drury, J. (2003). What critical psychology can('t) do for the anti-capitalist movement. *Annual Review of Critical Psychology, 3*, 88–113.

Eagleton, T. (2011). *Why Marx was right.* Yale University Press.

Enriquez, V. G. (1992). *From colonial to liberation psychology: The Philippine experience.* University of the Philippines Press.

Evans, S. D., Duckett, P., Lawthom, R., & Kivell, N. (2017). Positioning the critical in community psychology. In M. Bond, I. Serrano-Garcia, C. B. Keys, & M. Shinn (Eds.), *APA handbook of community psychology: Vol. 1. Theoretical foundations, core concepts, and emerging challenges (pp. 107–128).* American Psychological Association.

Fanon, F. (1963). *The wretched of the earth.* Grove Press.

Featherstone, D. (2012). *Solidarity: Hidden histories and geographies of internationalism.* Zed Books.

Fisher, M. (2009). *Capitalist realism: Is there no alternative?* Zero Books.

Fraser, N. (2014). Behind Marx's hidden abode. *New Left Review, 85*(2), 55–74.

Freire, P. (1972). *Pedagogy of the oppressed.* Herder and Herder.

Fryer, D. (2008). Some questions about "the history of community psychology". *Journal of Community Psychology, 36*(5), 572–586.

Galtung, J. (1969). Violence, peace, and peace research. *Journal of Peace Research, 6*(3), 167–191.

Gaztambide, D. (2019). *A people's history of psychoanalysis: From Freud to liberation psychology.* Lexington Books.

Gokani, R., & Walsh, R. T. (2017). On the historical and conceptual foundations of a community psychology of social transformation. *American Journal of Community Psychology, 59*(3–4), 284–294.

Hall, S. (1992). Cultural studies and its theoretical legacies. In L. Grossberg, C. Nelson, & P. Triechler (Eds.), *Cultural studies* (pp. 277–294). Routledge.

Hamber, B., Masilella, T. C., & Terre Blanche, M. (2001). Towards a Marxist community psychology: Radical tools for community psychological analysis and practice. In M. Seedat, S. Lazarus, & N. Duncan (Eds.), *Community psychology: Theory method and practice. South Africa and other perspectives (pp. 51–66).* Oxford University Press.

Hardt, M., & Negri, A. (2004). *Multitude.* Penguin Books.

Hardt, M., & Negri, A. (2009). *Commonwealth.* Harvard University Press.

Hardt, M., & Negri, A. (2017). *Assembly.* Oxford University Press.

Harvey, D. (2009). *Cosmopolitanism and the geographies of freedom*. Columbia University Press.

Harvey, D. (2020). *The anti-capitalist chronicles*. Pluto Press.

Hollander, N. C. (1997). *Love in a time of hate: Liberation psychology in Latin America*. Rutgers University Press.

Holloway, J. (2010). *Crack capitalism*. Pluto Press.

Javorka, M. (2021). Partnering with oppressive institutions for social change: Roles, ethics, and a framework for practicing accountability. *American Journal of Community Psychology, 68*(1–2), 3–17.

Kessi, S., Suffla, S., & Seedat, M. (2022). *Decolonial enactments in community psychology*. Springer.

Latham, R. (2018). Contemporary capitalism, uneven development, and the arc of anti-capitalism. *Global Discourse, 8*(2), 169–186.

Lazarus, S. (2018). *Power and identity in the struggle for social justice: Reflections on community psychology practice*. Springer.

Malherbe, N. (2018). Expanding conceptions of liberation: Holding Marxisms with liberation psychology. *Theory & Psychology, 28*(3), 340–357.

Malherbe, N. (2021). De-ideologization, liberation psychology, and the place of contradiction. *Journal for the Theory of Social Behaviour*. Advance online publication. https://doi.org/10.1111/jtsb.12322.

Malherbe, N., & Dlamini, S. (2020). Troubling history and diversity: Disciplinary decadence in community psychology. *Community Psychology in Global Perspective, 6*(2/1), 144–157.

Malherbe, N., Seedat, M., & Suffla, S. (2021). Analyzing discursive constructions of community in newspaper articles. *American Journal of Community Psychology, 67*(3–4), 433–446.

Malherbe, N., & Ratele, K. (2022). What and for whom is a decolonising African psychology? *Theory & Psychology, 32*(1), 116–130.

Martín, J. (2020). David Harvey against revolution: The bankruptcy of academic "Marxism". *Monthly Review*. Retrieved from https://www.marxist.com/david-harvey-against-revolution-the-bankruptcy-of-academic-marxism.htm

Martín-Baró, I. (1994). *Writings for a liberation psychology*. Harvard University Press.

Marx, K. (1977). *Capital: A critique of political economy* (Vol. 1). Vintage.

Marx, K. (1978a). Critique of the Gotha Programme. In R. Tucker (Ed.), *The Marx-Engels reader* (pp. 525–541). Norton.

Marx, K. (1978b). Theses on Feuerbach. In R. Tucker (Ed.), *The Marx-Engels reader* (pp. 143–145). Norton.

McGowan, T. (2019). *Emancipation after Hegel: Achieving a contradictory revolution*. Columbia University Press.

Melancholic Troglodytes. (2003). Anti-capitalism [Special Issue]. *Annual Review of Critical Psychology, 3*.

Montero, M. (1996). Parallel lives: Community psychology in Latin America and the United States. *American Journal of Community Psychology, 24*, 589–605.

Montero, M., & Sonn, C. C. (2009). About liberation and psychology: An introduction. In M. Montero & C. C. Sonn (Eds.), *Psychology of liberation* (pp. 1–10). Springer.

Montero, M., Sonn, C. C., & Burton, M. (2017). Community psychology and liberation psychology: A creative synergy for an ethical and transformative praxis. In M. A. Bond, I. Serrano-García, C. B. Keys, & M. Shinn (Eds.), *APA handbook of community psychology, Volume 1* (pp. 149–167). American Psychological Association.

Parker, I. (2009). Critical psychology and revolutionary Marxism. *Theory & Psychology, 19*, 71–92.

Parker, I. (2015). Politics and "applied psychology"? Theoretical concepts that question the disciplinary community. *Theory & Psychology, 25*(6), 719–734.

Pavón-Cuéllar, D. (2017). *Marxism and psychoanalysis: In or against psychology?* Routledge.

Pavón-Cuéllar, D., Moncada, L., & Painter, D. (2015). Marxism & psychology II [special issue]. *Annual Review of Critical Psychology, 12*.

Reich, S., Bishop, B., Carolissen, R., Dzidic, P., Portillo, N., Sasao, T., & Stark, W. (2017). Catalysis and connections: The (brief) history of community psychology throughout the world. In M. A. Bond, I. Serrano-García, & C. Keys (Eds.), *Handbook of community psychology volume 1: Theoretical foundations, core concepts, and emerging challenges* (pp. 21–66). American Psychological Association.

Sarason, S. B. (1974). *The psychological sense of community: Prospects for a community psychology*. Jossey-Bass.

Seedat, M., & Lazarus, S. (2011). Community psychology in South Africa: Origins, developments, and manifestations. *Journal of Community Psychology, 39*(3), 241–257.

Seedat, M., & Suffla, S. (2017a). Community psychology and its (dis)contents, archival legacies and decolonisation. *South Africa Journal of Psychology, 47*(4), 421–431.

Seedat, M., & Suffla, S. (2017b). Liberatory and critical voices in decolonising community psychology [special issue]. *South Africa Journal of Psychology, 47*(4).

Stevens, G. (2007). The international emergence and development of community psychology. In N. Duncan, B. Bowman, A. Naidoo, J. Pillay, & V. Roos (Eds.), *Community psychology: Analysis, context and action* (pp. 27–50). UCT Press.

Stevens, G., & Sonn, C. C. (2021). *Decoloniality and epistemic justice in contemporary community psychology*. Springer.

Tormey, S. (2004). *Anti-capitalism: A beginner's guide*. Oneworld.

Van Niekerk, A., Ratele, K., Seedat, M., & Suffla, S. (2014). How we learned to stop worrying and work with government. *Psychology in Society, 46,* 59–67.

Watkins, M., & Shulman, H. (2008). *Toward psychologies of liberation*. Palgrave Macmillan.

Watts, R. J., & Serrano-García, I. (2003). The quest for a liberating community psychology: An overview. *American Journal of Community Psychology, 31*(1), 73–78.

Wilkinson, E. (2017). On love as an (im)properly political concept. *Environment and Planning D: Society and Space, 35*(1), 57–71.

Wright, E. O. (2019). *How to be an anti-capitalist in the 21st century*. Verso.

Yeros, P., & Jha, P. (2020). Late neo-colonialism: Monopoly capitalism in permanent crisis. *Agrarian South: Journal of Political Economy, 9*(1), 78–93.

Žižek, S. (2018). *Like a thief in broad daylight: Power in the era of post-human capitalism*. Allen Lane.

Zlotowitz, S., & Burton, M. H. (2022). Community psychology and political economy. In C. Kagan, J. Akhurst, J. Alfaro, R. Lawthom, M. Richards, & A. Zambrano (Eds.), *The Routledge international handbook of community psychology: Facing global crises with hope* (pp. 46–59). Routledge.

Chapter 2
What Is Neoliberal Capitalism? Three Conceptions for an Anti-Capitalist Psychology of Community

It is not my intention in this chapter to historicise capitalism as a world economic system (some useful studies here include Federici, 2004; Hobsbawm, 1994; Patel & Moore, 2018; Rodney, 1972). Instead, in an attempt to delineate this book's central object of critique, I provide a necessarily incomplete sketch of capitalism as it exists today. This contemporary mode of capitalism is typically referred to as neoliberalism, or neoliberal capitalism. Before I flesh out what have, for me, been three helpful conceptions of neoliberalism, it is perhaps worth asking a question which, despite its simplicity, seems to resist a correspondingly simple answer: what is neoliberalism?

Wendy Brown (2015) has argued that neoliberalism is a loose signifier, which opens it up to many, often conflicting, interpretations. Some insist that this renders neoliberalism an analytically useless term (see, e.g. Boas & Gans-Morse, 2009; Phelps & White, 2018). If we cannot agree on what neoliberalism is, then how can it help us understand anything specific? While I believe that there is some merit to this view, I contend that the term neoliberalism can, in fact, be useful for critical analyses in two central ways. Firstly, because neoliberalism is a loose—rather than an empty—signifier, it remains a dynamic term that is always locked into capitalism's contemporary conjuncture. It is, therefore, a term that is attentive to the movement of capital. Indeed, as we shall see, contemporary capitalism does not function in the same way everywhere. Part of its pervasive power lies in the fact that it has not reached a settled form (Latham, 2018). Yet, it still retains several core features, and the loose composition of the term neoliberalism—which implies a general form without fixed content—is useful for addressing the dynamism of today's capitalism. Secondly, neoliberalism, slippery as the term is, allows us to understand and approach capitalism as a multifarious and layered system. This, I argue, can inform and strengthen multi-pronged anti-capitalist resistance politics that seek to attack capitalism at several different points. It is for these two reasons that I prefer neoliberalism to a term like "late capitalism" (see Mandel, 1979) which seems, to me at least, to rather optimistically anticipate the end of capitalism without grappling with the ever-shifting expansiveness of capitalism's present-day movements, valances, and formations. Although neoliberalism cannot explain everything (Brown, 2019), it can provide insights into an oppressive global order that must be resisted and remade if we are to free ourselves of the tyrannical grip that neoliberalism exerts over so many aspects of our lives (Malherbe, 2018).

N. Malherbe, *For an Anti-capitalist Psychology of Community*, Community Psychology, https://doi.org/10.1007/978-3-030-99696-3_2

Let us return to our central question: what is neoliberalism? Since its emergence in the 1970s, neoliberalism has been characterised by the rolling back of social insurance; a reduction in taxes and associated public goods; the deregulation of production and markets; the protection of corporate power; a reduction in redistributive State interventions; the weakening of trade unions (and, therefore, the disempowerment of labour more generally); cutbacks to finance and environmental regulations; and the privatisation (and consequent undermining of the quality and character) of State services (Brown, 2015, 2019; Wright, 2019). In these ways, neoliberalism has seen political and economic resources mobilised to assure as much wealth and power as possible for the corporate class (Harvey, 2020). Brown (2015) has argued that by placing minimal constraints on the movement of global capital (which, following Marx, we might define as *value in motion*; see Harvey, 2005, 2017) and by deregulating the financial sector, neoliberal policies have ensured that States are more attentive to the interests of finance than they are to the needs of citizens. This has, in turn, undermined social power. Democracy has become understood merely in terms of voting and civil rights, rather than a process by which to attend to people's wellbeing (Brown, 2019). Moreover, neoliberalism's "aggressive affirmation and enforcement of private property rights" (Wright, 2015, p. 237) have had dire effects not only on people's quality of life but also on public life. The globalisation and financialisation of neoliberal orthodoxy have weakened the resistance capacities of labour and social movements by increasing wealth inequality and bolstering the bargaining power of capital (Wright, 2019). This has been especially detrimental in the Global South, where neoliberalism has ushered in a new age of extractive neo-imperialism (Amin, 2014a; Nkrumah, 1965; Yeros & Jha, 2020). In light of all of this, we can understand neoliberalism as a kind of structural violence (see Galtung, 1969).

Neoliberalism has not, however, been implemented uniformly. It has been uneven in its rollout (Latham, 2018), differing across space and time (Harvey, 2005). We see this unevenness in the ways that neoliberalism has interacted with different cultures, histories, and social circumstances, such as South Africa's post-apartheid reforms, India's Hindu nationalism, China's State socialism, and different authoritarian regimes in places like Brazil, Chile, Turkey, and Hungary. However, the uneven nature of neoliberalism is perhaps most evident in its relationship with imperialism (i.e. using capital to control economic territories, including the land, labour, resources, and minerals of these territories, Ghosh, 2021). Samir Amin (2014a) has argued that, since the emergence of neoliberalism, the falling rate of growth in the capitalist centres has resulted in an intensification of imperialist rent (i.e. workers in the Global South earning less than those in the North, despite producing the same value) as well as the domination—on a global scale—of what he calls the imperialist triad, namely, the United States, Europe, and Japan (some would add China to this triad, but this has been contested; see Ghosh, 2021). Amin (2014a) goes on to recount how imperialist rent and the imperialist triad have monopolised the world capitalist economy through technology, access to natural resources, finance, the global media, and the means of mass destruction (see also Amin, 2014b). In this, neoliberalism has weakened the autonomous development of the Global South while worsening the economic conditions for all workers and small-scale producers (Ghosh, 2021).

In what follows, I outline three interlinked conceptions of neoliberal capitalism, namely, neoliberalism as a political project, an ideology, and a normative rationality. These are certainly not the only ways of approaching neoliberalism. Simon Springer (2012), for instance, has argued that neoliberalism constitutes a discourse, whereas Jamie Peck (2001) insists that it is a type of State that is invested in the protection of capital. Nancy Fraser (2014), on the other hand, argues that it is an institutionalised social order. However, rather than argue against interpretations of neoliberalism which differ from my own, I have attempted to subsume some (but, of course, not all) of them into my own analysis. Springer's (2012) neoliberal discourse, for example, is reflected in my consideration of neoliberal ideology, just as Peck's (2001) notion of the neoliberal State is subsumed in my understanding of neoliberalism as a political project, whereas Fraser's (2014) notion of a neoliberal institutional social order cuts across each of the three conceptions of neoliberalism that I consider. My aim, then, is not to argue against or for a specific approach to understanding neoliberalism (see Mandel, 1979), but to engage neoliberalism in a way that reflects a multitude of approaches that might be useful for those working within what I am calling an anti-capitalist psychology of community.

These three conceptions of neoliberalism (as a political project, an ideology, and a normative rationality) should not be understood as functioning independent from one another. As Erik Olin Wright (2015) argues, "A society is not a system in the same way that an organism is a system. It is more like the loosely coupled system of an ecosystem in which a variety of processes interact in relatively contingent ways" (p. 121). Together, these conceptions of neoliberalism can assist us in understanding the complex socio-political processes by which capitalist society is constituted. However, it is difficult to attack the neoliberal political project, neoliberal ideology, and neoliberal rationality all at once. It is because anti-capitalist resistance is unable to take on the totality of capitalism that it is useful to enter into anti-capitalism through either politics, ideology, or normative rationality and from here seek to connect with and address other formations of anti-capitalist resistance that can, together, work to erode capitalism (see Wright, 2019). Within solidarity-building efforts, for instance, neoliberal ideology is an important consideration, whereas for anti-capitalist consciousness-raising groups, neoliberalism's normative rationality will be especially salient; and for social reproduction struggles, it is the neoliberal political project that will take centre stage. A powerful and cohesive anti-capitalist movement will thus incorporate and make links between all three of these approaches. To neatly separate neoliberal capitalism (and anti-capitalist resistance) into politics, ideology, and normative rationality is, therefore, artificial, but it is also tactical and analytically useful.

In the remainder of this chapter, I outline the three aforementioned conceptions of neoliberal capitalism, after which I consider how each relates to the other, arguing for an expansive anti-capitalism that engages the political, ideological, and rationalising character of capitalism. I then offer a brief sketch of how mainstream community psychology has aligned with and been shaped by neoliberal capitalism and conclude by emphasising the imperative of an anti-capitalist psychology of community.

Neoliberal Capitalism as a Political Project

The resurgence of the rather orthodox Marxian understanding of neoliberalism as a consciously constructed political project is indebted in great part to the work of David Harvey (Brown, 2015). It is, however, important that we incorporate theories of feminism and coloniality into this Marxist view so that we can grasp the imperialist, patriarchal nature of the neoliberal political project (Fraser et al., 2019; Ndlovu-Gatsheni, 2021). "Stretching" Marxist theory in these ways enables us to recognise not only how neoliberalism commodifies labouring bodies but also how it brutalises gendered and racialised bodies (Hardt & Negri, 2009).

In the 1970s, the neoliberal political project emerged in the United States and the United Kingdom as a response to the capitalist State's crisis of legitimacy. More specifically, between 1973 and 1982, global capitalism saw a major reconstruction which aligned, in large part, with the Austrian and Chicago Schools of Economics as well as German Ordoliberalism (see Harvey, 2017; Saad-Filho, 2017). This reconstruction represented a reaction to the weakening of capitalist class power as well as lagging capitalist accumulation—particularly in the United States—due to the relative success of labour struggles and other social movements (Brown, 2015; Harvey, 2005). As Harvey (2005, 2017) demonstrates, capitalist States, in conjunction with major corporations and mainstream media, sought to re-empower capital through deindustrialisation (which ensured the precarity of labour) as well as offshoring and organisational changes (e.g. subcontracting and outsourcing). Thus, in an attempt to boost declining profits, ruling elites—particularly in the capitalist centres (see Amin, 2010)—carried out public policies that repressed wages and reduced State provisions. This sort of neoliberal public policy, which remains dominant today, can be surmised by what Steger and Roy (2021) refer to as the DLP formula: Deregulation of industry; Liberalisation of trade; and Privatisation of State-owned enterprises.

For the neoliberal project, accumulation is underwritten by, but not reducible to, what is known as financialisation (Fine & Saad-Filho, 2017). We see financialisation in how interest-bearing capital determines the allocation of social resources through distinct forms of fictitious capital (Saad-Filho, 2017). Although this might seem distant from the realities of our day-to-day lives, it is because of this abstraction that we do not always recognise how finance binds us into debt and constrains production activity (Amin, 2010; Hardt & Negri, 2009), including social reproduction which, under neoliberalism, remains feminised and under-valued (Fraser et al., 2019). Finance functions, effectively, as a claim on our future labour, locking us into debt peonage (Harvey, 2020). Industrial firms have become increasingly dependent on financialised—rather than industrial—profits, meaning that debt has ballooned among corporations, governments, and households, resulting in the systematic inflation of asset prices as well as falling profits in production (Yeros & Jha, 2020).

Neoliberalism draws on the power of the State to impose, drive, underwrite, and manage the internationalisation of the production of finance in almost all aspects of our daily lives (Harvey, 2017; Saad-Filho, 2017). The State has, in this sense, moved away from supporting people to supporting enterprise through tax arrangements, subsidies, and the evasion of regulations (Harvey, 2020). This is thought to work better than democratic processes and State guidance (Saad-Filho, 2017). Yet, the State also manages production and finance and employs its monopoly on violence to protect neoliberal interests (Harvey, 2005), meaning that actually existing neoliberalism often contrasts with its purported values of minimal State intervention (Brown, 2019). The financialisation that defines the neoliberal political project has, in recent years, aligned with right-wing populism (Harvey, 2020; Kotsko, 2018)— and even (neo)fascism—in the ways it defends accumulation (see also Césaire, 1972; Yeros & Jha, 2020). As such, neoliberalism has shown to be perfectly capable of functioning without the democratic principles it espouses (see Brown, 2015) and thus does not require the support of any specific political form (Hardt & Negri, 2009).

Financialisation is, for the most part, concentrated in the Global North. The financial power of neoliberalism as a political project depends on the physical production of commodities in the Global South (Amin, 2010). The expansion of the neoliberal project depends on extracting resources from colonies precisely because industry can only incorporate a limited number of people (Amin, 1989, 2010). Since the inception of neoliberal reforms, States within the capitalist centres have sought to create new markets by appropriating the assets and natural resources of former colonies, devastating them in the process (see Amin, 1989, 2010; Harvey, 2017). We saw this during the onset of neoliberalism, where transnational institutions like the World Bank and the International Monetary Fund sought to disseminate neoliberalism in a manner that mimicked the economic mechanisms of imperialism (Brown, 2019), with some of the earliest "experiments" in neoliberalism undertaken in the Global South (e.g. the 1974 US-backed installation of the Pinochet dictatorship in Chile). Like earlier modalities of capitalism, the foundations of the neoliberal project are to be found in imperialist and racist extractivism (Amin, 1989), which has resulted in colonised knowledges, the enclosure of land, as well as the imposition of private property rights and wage labour (see Harvey, 2020; Ndlovu-Gatsheni, 2021). It is in these ways that neoliberalism destroys its principal sources of wealth: human beings and nature (Amin, 2014b).

In many places, such as South Africa and Brazil, neoliberalism allowed for a transition to neocolonialism whereby powers in the capitalist centres were able to maintain economic and social control over former colonies via indirect rule (Yeros & Jha, 2020). This situation was anticipated by anti-imperialist thinkers like Frantz Fanon (1963) and Kwame Nkrumah (1965), who predicted that after independence, former colonies would remain governed by imperial economic mechanisms, only now these mechanisms would be managed by a local elite (see also Ndlovu-Gatsheni, 2021; Yeros & Jha, 2020). Neo-imperialism, therefore, does not denote one country versus another, but rather capital versus people everywhere (Ghosh, 2021). As such, Marx's (1977) notion of original accumulation is mistaken in its assertion that a nakedly violent form of accumulation (which separates producers from the means of production, Holloway, 2010) was only present at the dawn of capitalism. Violence, it seems, is fundamental to the functioning of today's neoliberal capitalist project, with its dependence on war, land grabs, vaccine profiteering, dispossession, mineral extraction, as well as privatisation of the commons, public services, and genetic material (Hardt & Negri, 2009; Harvey, 2020; Yeros & Jha, 2020). Original accumulation has not disappeared. It has changed its form and continues to be reproduced daily (see Ghosh, 2021; Shalhoub-Kevorkian & Wahab, 2021).

Perhaps the key event in the development of the neoliberal political project was the breakdown of the Bretton Woods System[1] in 1971, which enabled the United States to finance its deficits and monopolies with very few constraints (Yeros & Jha, 2020) and ensured that local economies no longer functioned as closed systems, with working people—all over the world—now in competition with one another (Harvey, 2020). This unfettered capitalist expansion solidified the power of the United States to exercise monopoly control over finance capital by draining the capitalist peripheries of land, resources, and labour; reducing compensation for working people in the capitalist centres; escalating colonial intervention; manipulating conflict situations in the peripheries; and inventing strategic enemies to justify warfare that segregates the world and its resources (Amin, 2010; Hardt & Negri, 2009; Nkrumah, 1965; Yeros & Jha, 2020). Although the hyper-imperialist capacities of the United States have, today, diminished somewhat since the 1970s and 1980s, the United States remains neoliberalism's principle neocolonial power (Ghosh, 2021).

In essence, when we conceptualise neoliberal capitalism as a political project, we are speaking of an effort, beginning in the 1970s, on the part of elites to restore class power and to use economic crises to wrest back control of the global economy and, subsequently, society (see Brown, 2015; Harvey, 2005). In this view, neoliberalism embodies the present-day modality of capitalism which has been carried out by those State policies, institutions, and practices that have led a ruling class offensive against the poor by redistributing wealth and income upwards (Saad-Filho, 2017), oftentimes through neocolonial mechanisms of extraction (Yeros & Jha, 2020). Although ideology has been acknowledged as an important component of the neoliberal project (Harvey, 2005), for many, ideology represents the defining feature of neoliberal capitalism.

Neoliberal Capitalism as an Ideology

Esposito and Perez (2014) argue that instead of conceiving of neoliberalism as a political project, we can approach it as an ensemble of ideological forces that displace the structural, interconnected nature of capitalist society through an intensely individualised reading of reality. However, conceptualising neoliberalism as an ideology is not without its theoretical problems. Throughout history, ideology has

---

[1] Established in 1944, the Bretton Woods System denoted an agreement among the central banks to maintain fixed exchange rates between local currencies and the US dollar (Harvey, 2020).

taken on several—sometimes incompatible—meanings (see Eagleton, 1991), which makes mapping a distinctive *neoliberal ideology* an especially complicated task. For our purposes though, it may be useful to begin with the highly influential Marxian formulation of ideology which, of course, predates neoliberal ideology, but nonetheless offers us several insights for understanding it.

Marx and Engels (1970) wrote that ideology denotes the dominant ideas in a society. These ideas, they argued, are determined by the ruling classes (i.e. those who own, manage, and control the means of production as well as surplus value), meaning that ideology always has a material basis. As they describe it in a well-known passage:

> [T]he ideas of the ruling class are in every epoch the ruling ideas, i.e. the class which is the ruling material force of society, is at the same time its ruling intellectual force. The class which has the means of material production at its disposal has control at the same time over the means of mental production, so that thereby, generally speaking, the ideas of those who lack the means of mental production are subject to it. (Marx & Engels, 1970, p. 64)

Ideology, for orthodox Marxists, works by obscuring the class antagonisms of capitalist society by making these antagonisms appear cultural, psychological, and/or subjective. Put differently, because we can understand the laws of capitalism, that which functions to deny this understanding is ideological and should be replaced with the "true knowledge" that emerges in class struggle (see Glynos, 2001). Yet, as we have seen, neoliberal capitalism has taken on a much more pervasive form than the capitalism of Marx's day. As such, neoliberal ideology is not singular or coherent. It is attached to an unstable and ever-shifting spectrum of ideas (Fine & Saad-Filho, 2017). Therefore, any attempt to understand neoliberal ideology must bring the Marxian notion of ideology to bear on our contemporary conjuncture.

In his treatise on the dialectic, Todd McGowan (2019) offers a useful formulation of ideology that we can apply to neoliberal ideology more specifically. He defines ideology as the social processes which make inherent contradictions appear to us as external oppositions, thereby concealing and repressing the internal tensions of a subject, system, or object (see also Therborn, 1980). For example, when viewed through an ideological lens, capitalists and workers appear to confront each other in an external relationship (rather than within a contradictory, mutually constitutive one), and in this way, contradictions (i.e. how the interests of workers and capitalists coalesce to form capitalism's internal instability) are made to seem like differences that exist independent from one another (Malherbe, 2021b). How, then, is neoliberal ideology distinctive from a more general capitalist ideology? The answer to this lies in the way that neoliberal ideology leverages personal responsibility to obscure how capitalist wealth is generated by the exploitation of the majority. The economic success of an individual is thereby attributed solely to that individual. To put this more technically, meritocracy (i.e. the myth that society rewards those who are most talented or who work hardest, no matter their circumstances) functions as the quilting point of neoliberal ideology, which is to say, meritocracy serves as the point at which neoliberal ideology—as a system of signification—attains meaning and seeming coherence (see Žižek, 1989).

Understanding how neoliberal ideology works requires that we understand how ideology more generally produces subjectivities, that is, how the self is constituted as a psychological agent within society (Therborn, 1980). Thus, although ideology hails us as subjects, we are always also misrecognised by ideology. The subjectivities offered to us appear to be whole, coherent, meaningful, and reasonable, and as such, there is no recognition or space made for the ways by which we do not identify with these subjectivities (i.e. our subjective contradictions). Ideology's fixity, in other words, means that it fails to symbolise the self in its ever-shifting totality (Glynos, 2001). For instance, as a man, there are myriad ways by which I do not identify with the dominant, most readily available ideologies of masculinity. It is because ideology consistently misrecognises the subject in this way that individuals tend to feel alienated (Malherbe, 2021a, b).

For the neoliberal subject, to fail economically is to fail subjectively. Although there are, of course, variations within neoliberal subjectivities (Teo, 2018), these subjectivities tend to map onto the neoliberal order, with successful subjectivity obtained via the individual's reading of market signals, capacity to produce quantifiable outputs, and/or ability to turn a profit (Esposito & Perez, 2014). The subject's self-actualisation is dependent on achieving economic success in a global economic system that, by design, can bestow success of this kind onto very few individuals. When the subject's sense of morality, self, and the social good is measured against the capitalist economy, the very notion of ethics comes to denote little more than the free market and market-directed activity (Ailon, 2022), which, once again, exacerbates feelings of alienation (Malherbe, 2021a).

The ways by which individuals do not identify with the subjectivities imposed onto them by neoliberal ideology are made to seem pathological (see Esposito & Perez, 2014; Malherbe, 2021b). In this regard, neoliberal ideology produces desire within subjects by telling them how to desire in accordance with a particular subjectivity (Glynos, 2001). These desires are bound to perpetually unsatisfying consumer choices which re-present our unfreedom to us in the guise of freedom of choice (Žižek, 2020). Marx (1977) spoke of this situation as being defined by the fetishised commodity, whereby people look to commodities to deliver them from the alienating subjectivities offered by capitalism. That which is sold to us is pressed into us emotionally, and we repress the fact that the commodity embodies capitalist exploitation, our own and that of others (Fromm, 1942). The fleeting solace that we attain from the false wholeness offered by neoliberal subjectivities and commodities is crucial for securing our consent to, investment in, and perpetuation of the neoliberal ideological order (Harvey, 2005; Žižek, 1989).

In her study, Brown (2006) demonstrates that since the 1980s, neoliberal ideology has functioned in large part through what she calls liberal tolerance. Tolerance of this kind stresses that the social antagonisms fostered by neoliberalism (i.e. tensions which arise from neoliberal ideology's emphasis on competition for resources and the personal responsibility for failing to secure these resources for oneself and/or one's family) are to be understood as psychological, natural, and/or cultural conflicts that can be overcome by tolerating one another as well as the socioeconomic order that produces these antagonisms. The political and the material are thus individualised, and the unregulated free market is looked to as a kind of impartial cultural mediator (Malherbe, 2020). Exemplary here are corporate diversity programmes that celebrate difference at the expense of grappling with power inequalities, managing antagonisms to hail a docile citizenry (see Brown, 2006). In turn, we are encouraged to turn away from struggles for equality and justice and towards a tolerant attitude of permissiveness and resignation (Brown, 2006, 2015). Slavoj Žižek (2020) reminds us, however, that neoliberal ideology's emphasis on tolerance is not as permissive as it might appear. It brutally excludes anti-capitalist insurgence and, in so doing, impinges on our ability to conceive of a better world. It is, therefore, a tolerance with intensely policed boundaries or what we might think of as repressive tolerance (see Wolff et al., 1965).

Neoliberal ideology does not, however, promote liberal/repressive tolerance in every instance. On the contrary, Terry Eagleton (1991) has argued that the power of an ideology—neoliberalism included—lies in its capacity to divide societies. We see neoliberalism's divisive power in the way that outgroups are constructed through racist, xenophobic, and/or sexist discourse so that they appear to be preventing ingroups from attaining full satisfaction (see McGowan, 2019; Žižek, 1989). Put differently, the Other is established as obstructing the self from achieving the unified subjectivity promised by neoliberal ideology (Malherbe, 2021b). In this sense, neoliberal ideology locates the Other in what Fanon (1967) refers to as the zone of nonbeing, wherein the Other's humanity is denied. When placed in this zone of nonbeing, the Other's existence is defined by and equated with violence which, in turn, justifies violent action taken against the Other. We see this on a global scale where enemies are invented to vindicate near-permanent warfare and neoliberal imperialist intervention in the capitalist peripheries (Amin, 2010; Césaire, 1972; Yeros & Jha, 2020). It should, however, be noted that although ideological relations between people are not in and of themselves grounded in material reality, ideology typically emerges from people's real experiences (see Malherbe, 2021b; Therborn, 1980). For example, the threat of the foreign Other, which scaffolds xenophobic attitudes, is not real, but the economic precarity out of which these attitudes arise—for so many—is, indeed, real in a material sense. To understand neoliberal ideology thus requires that we examine its material and structural roots.

For neoliberal ideology, freedom depends on individual responsibility rather than the ability of social structures to ensure freedom through, for example, affordable and reliable healthcare (Malherbe, 2021b). As such, freedom becomes burdensome for the individual subject, denoting little more than individual choice, competition, personal duty, and private pursuits (Esposito & Perez, 2014). In his well-known thesis, Erich Fromm (1942) describes how people may wish to escape from this kind of freedom through the more constraining (and seemingly protective) dictates of fascist ideology. Moreover, neoliberal ideology's emphasis on consumption and individual responsibility often translates into a demand from the big Other (i.e. an imagined social authority, Malherbe, 2021a) to enjoy ourselves as much as possible (Žižek, 1989, 2020). This command to enjoy is, however, also burdensome. The constant pressure to consume or transgress in ways that bolster the neoliberal order is, for many, unbearable. Neoliberal ideology's compulsion to enjoy, coupled with its confinement of freedom to personal responsibility, has resulted in enormously high rates of depression and burnout (Han, 2017).

Neoliberal ideology informs how we make sense of contradictory experiences (Eagleton, 1991; Žižek, 2020). However, as Žižek (1989) argues, even though we know that neoliberal ideology is false or at least based on fundamental falsehoods, we adhere to it anyway. Our adherence to neoliberal ideology is, therefore, not necessarily the product of a deluded "false consciousness", as many Marxists would have it, but rather a fear of retribution from the State or employers (Therborn, 1980) and/or the need to cope with and make sense of subjective and societal contradictions, many of which are too traumatic to face directly (McGowan, 2019). It is for these reasons that neoliberal ideology has, today, accrued what Antonio Gramsci (1971) referred to as hegemony, whereby power is—for the most part—exercised not through direct coercion (although, as highlighted earlier, neoliberalism will resort to violent coercion and even fascism if need be, Harvey, 2020; Yeros & Jha, 2020), but through meritocratic values (e.g. competitive individualism and personal responsibility for systemic failure) to which people consent, either actively or passively due to a lack of alternatives (see Chibber, 2022). Subjective normality is thereby measured with reference to one's adherence to these hegemonic values (Esposito & Perez, 2014). Discrediting neoliberal ideology is difficult precisely because it renders meritocracy commonsensical (Amin, 2010; Eagleton, 1991; Harvey, 2020; McGowan, 2019). This common sense is undergirded by an economistic rationality that, for some, denotes the core component of neoliberal capitalism.

Neoliberal Capitalism as Normative Rationality

The work of Wendy Brown (2015, 2019) has been instrumental in conceptualising neoliberalism as a kind of normative rationality. Brown, herself, draws heavily on Michele Foucault's (2010) notion of biopolitics; however, she is also critical of Foucault, noting the inadequate attention that he pays to democracy and capital (we could add to this his insufficient analysis of and his unwillingness to name imperialism, coloniality, and patriarchy). Thus, in trying to understand what Brown means by neoliberal capitalism as a normative rationality, we must first delineate what Foucault meant by biopolitics. Refracting the material and the discursive through one another (Springer, 2012), biopolitical practices denote the capacities of the capitalist State (which, in Foucault's time, was still emerging as a neoliberal State) to use human bodies for purposes of governance, that is, for political and economic control. Biopolitics, in other words, indicates how subjects are governed at the bodily level through soft power and common sense (Brown, 2015; Han, 2017). In turn, people make history and subjectivities with, against, and through biopolitical antagonisms and the power systems in which these antagonisms are lodged (Hardt & Negri, 2009). Yet, as Achille Mbembe (2019) notes, biopolitics is not always appropriate for studying the ways by which neoliberal rationality coalescences with coloniality.[2] He argues instead for the notion of necropolitics, whereby the normative capitalist order is premised on determining who matters, who does not, and which lives are disposable (see also Shalhoub-Kevorkian & Wahab, 2021). Put differently, necropolitics—which is structured by the historical trajectory of colonial rule—denotes governance via an economy of death, where the lives of some (e.g. the lives of Black, poor, indigenous, transgender women) are made into killable sites so that the lives of others (e.g. the lives of White, wealthy, able-bodied, cisgender men) can be valued and preserved. Both necropolitics and biopolitics emphasise the subordinated place of the body—or particular bodies—within the ruling neoliberal order, thus influencing seemingly rational perceptions of the body's meaning and purpose.

Through biopolitical and necropolitical practices, neoliberalism comes into our understanding not as a political project or an ideology, but as a mode of normative rationality. A rationality of this sort, Brown (2015) demonstrates, has altered life in accordance with the economic, which is to say that the logic of capital has, today, been unleashed into areas where it was not always welcome (Brown, 2019; Fine & Saad-Filho, 2017). When all of life, and the human bodies which comprise and make this life, is framed by neoliberal rationality, nearly everything is perceived in terms of economic metrics, even when not directly monetised. Neoliberal rationalities are, in this sense, "world-changing, hegemonic orders of normative reason, generative of subjects, markets, states, law, jurisprudence, and their relations" (Brown, 2015, p. 121). From this arises what Carl Ratner (2019) has called neoliberal semiotics, which sees the marketisation of language, wherein human relations are recast in commercial terms (e.g. those who use public transport are "customers" rather than people or citizens). Similarly, when couched in neoliberal rationality, oppressive capitalist practices can be rebranded as empowering. Micro-lending, for instance, is touted as improving the lives of those in the Global South, rather than plunging them further into debt peonage (Brown, 2019; Harvey, 2020).

Brown (2015) writes that "Neoliberalism is the rationality through which capitalism finally swallows humanity" (p. 44), binding human life to the production of wealth and establishing a normative order of reason that operates through economising truth regimes (see Foucault, 2010). We see this today in the rise of the so-called gig economy, where workers are encouraged to be marketable "entrepreneurs of the self" without any benefits or protections (Žižek, 2020). To use Foucauldian language (see Foucault, 2010), neoliberal rationality renders the human subject *homo economicus* (which could be updated today as *homo neoliberalus*, Teo, 2018), a non-relational subjectivity wherein each individual is read as a piece of human capital to be bought, sold, and marketed (Brown, 2015). Homo economicus acts in terms of value enhancement, self-interest, and attaining utilitarian knowledge (Esposito & Perez, 2014) and as such engages both the self and others

[2] In his well-known definition, Nelson Maldonado-Torres (2007) describes coloniality as the "long-standing patterns of power that emerged as a result of colonialism, but that define culture, labor, intersubjective relations, and knowledge production well beyond the strict limits of colonial administrations. Thus, coloniality survives colonialism" (p. 240).

instrumentally which, in turn, intensifies feelings of alienation as relations between people are made to seem like relations between things (see Marx, 1977). Human life is, in this regard, cheapened and made small (see Patel & Moore, 2018), with agency limited to a reductive exercise of entrepreneurial freedom within an industrialised framework (Harvey, 2005, 2017). Like neoliberal ideology, neoliberal rationality renders inequality, mass poverty, colonial destruction, and imperialism the products of those units of human capital that did not successfully compete with others (Wark, 2017).

Neoliberal rationality's repeated emphasis on the economised, marketable subject undermines democracy, with the so-called free market serving as the principal operation of the State (Wark, 2017). The political character of democracy is, in this regard, made into an economic matter, with popular sovereignty (i.e. democracy on the margins; see Ngwane, 2021) erased or ignored so that corporate power can be bolstered and legitimised (Brown, 2019). The State and its security apparatuses are, in other words, activated on behalf of the neoliberal economy, rather than the people who keep this economy going. In this, governments act merely to promote economic growth and improve investment climates (Brown, 2015; Harvey, 2020). States are, therefore, not held accountable to communities, with State processes (especially necropolitical processes) made opaque and untransparent (Shalhoub-Kevorkian & Wahab, 2021). As such, neoliberal rationality does not originate in the State. It circulates through and is implemented by the State (Wark, 2017).

In addition to debasing democracy in favour of free-market logic, neoliberal rationality can also appeal to what is called "traditional morality", which includes patriarchal human relations, coloniality, and even religious fundamentalism (Brown, 2019). Rhetoric based on traditional morality seeks to undermine civil liberties by holding up a static conception of "tradition" as that which can provide order and morality to a chaotic present (see Malherbe, 2020). Progress, somewhat paradoxically, then becomes associated with a valourised notion of tradition that is steeped in colonial and patriarchal violence (Césaire, 1972), with the free market heralded as a moral good (Kotsko, 2018). For instance, in what Samir Amin (1989) refers to as Eurocentrism, science, human rights, progress, and democracy are positioned by neoliberal rationality as having been developed in—and are the sole products of—Europe and (White, usually male) Europeans. In this way, neoliberal colonial extractivism is held up as a gift that has been bestowed to the Global South (see Ndlovu-Gatsheni, 2021), functioning merely to increase benevolent market influence and democracy (Yeros & Jha, 2020). Similarly, neoliberal rationality appeals to traditional morality when social reproduction (i.e. work that attends to the emotional and physical needs of others) is rendered the moral duty of women (Fraser, 2014; Fraser et al., 2019). Rationalising social reproduction in this way justifies the under- or non-waged status of this kind of labour, despite its centrality in sustaining human life (Hardt & Negri, 2009). The starkly racist and sexist forms that neoliberal rationality assumes when grounded in traditional morality should not, however, be understood as entirely different from the more "liberal" variants of neoliberal rationality. Rather, each represents an alternative approach to activating neoliberalism as normative rationality (see Kotsko, 2018).

Capitalist production is, today, interested in not only commodities but also emotion, social relations, and forms of life (Hardt & Negri, 2009), and it is these seemingly immaterial facets of our lives with which neoliberal rationality is especially concerned. Therefore, although I have thus far outlined homo economicus in relation to Foucault's (2010) biopolitics and Mbembe's (2019) necropolitics, we can also understand homo economicus as being produced through what Byung-Chul Han (2017) calls psychopolitics, whereby selling and marketing the self relies on the evocation of positive emotions (e.g. the attention we receive on social media). In this, our emotions are exploited and managed not only to sell products but also to ensure that our lives are monitored through a consensual kind of auto-surveillance. Yet, whether conceived through biopolitics, necropolitics, or psychopolitics, neoliberal rationality calls on the subject to remain autonomous and self-managing while, at the same time, obeying State commands (sometimes with a smile). We are, in other words, allowed to exercise individual freedoms insofar as these freedoms follow market discipline (Wark, 2017).

Neoliberal rationality casts an economising interpretive frame over almost all facets of our lives (Brown, 2015), with our material needs, spiritual requirements, romantic interests, and personal safety made into articles of commerce to be purchased and sold in the marketplace (Esposito & Perez, 2014). Neoliberal rationality is neither top-down nor bottom-up. It is a circuitry process of socioeconomic and spatial transformation that engenders in people an unfreedom that operates through guises of permissiveness, agency, and self-actualisation (Springer, 2012; Žižek, 2020). In Brown's (2015) words, neoliberal rationality "governs as sophisticated common sense" (p. 35), a common sense that is derived from organising society, the bodies which comprise it, and morality through a marketised logic that can be readily mapped onto colonial and patriarchal social structures which have always functioned by cheapening certain lives, affects, bodies, and labours (Brown, 2019; Patel & Moore, 2018; Yeros & Jha, 2020).

Developing an Expansive Conception of Neoliberal Capitalism

In the above sections, I offer three conceptions of neoliberal capitalism, that is, neoliberalism as a political project, an ideology, and a normative rationality. Developing an expansive conception of neoliberalism, however, does not require that we understand the above three conceptions as operating alongside one another in the formation of a coherent whole (i.e. three equal slices that comprise the neoliberal pie). Rather, I argue, approaching neoliberalism expansively necessitates an analysis of the different connections between neoliberal politics, ideology, and rationality. These connections can be illustrative precisely because they are not static. They are always formed and reformed within specific conjunctures as well as in response to crises of and resistances to neoliberalism (see Fine & Saad-Filho, 2017). Thus, even when we focus on one conception of neoliberalism, the others are not muted or put to one side. At different moments and in different ways, each conception reinforces, shapes, strengthens, and contradicts the others (see Steger & Roy, 2021). Scholars such as Wright (2019) are at pains to point out that neoliberal ideology, for instance, was designed and implemented for the express purpose of justifying the neoliberal political project which, in turn, produces the neoliberal rationality that structures our day-to-day perceptions. It is, therefore, together that these three conceptions of neoliberalism emphasise how the material and the discursive are mutually constitutive within neoliberal capitalism (see Springer, 2012), with broadly appealing notions like "individual freedom", "competition", and "democracy" serving as empty signifiers that justify finance-based policies and State practices (Saad-Filho, 2017), as well as guide an economising hegemony (Harvey, 2005, 2020).

The expansive approach to neoliberalism that I am advocating here (i.e. one that stresses the continually shifting connections between politics, ideology, and rationality, rather than the singular coherence of all three) is useful in that it enables us to understand the structural characteristics of neoliberalism in a way that does not deny human agency (see Springer, 2012). All over the world and across the political spectrum, people have resisted the near omnipotence of neoliberalism. Thus, although neoliberalism has unquestionably narrowed the scope for debate and—through systematising the precarity of life and labour—made anti-capitalist contestation especially difficult (Fine & Saad-Filho, 2017; Saad-Filho, 2017), we should not understand neoliberalism as foreclosed. It contains within it ruptures, contradictions, and antagonisms that can be seized upon. When we approach neoliberalism in the expansive manner that I am suggesting, we become aware of the multiple points into which anti-capitalist action can enter. As John Holloway (2010) argues, "cracking" capitalism does not mean locating a single fissure within its structure. It requires instead that we break capitalism "in as many ways as we can and try to expand and multiply the cracks and promote their confluence" (Holloway, 2010, p. 11). In this, we may act to not only sever neoliberalism from within but also make connections between different anti-capitalisms. In approaching neoliberalism in such an expansive manner, the anti-capitalist project is able to take on necessarily ambitious forms.

Community Psychology and Neoliberal Capitalism

Before I flesh out some of the ways by which an anti-capitalist psychology of community can address itself to neoliberalism, it is worth touching on how community psychology has been shaped by neoliberalism. I focus here on community psychology because it is the branch of formalised psychology that most informs what I am calling a psychology of community (see Chap. 1). My intention here is not to disregard community psychology altogether, but to engage critically with the disciplinary context against and within which many who practise an anti-capitalist psychology of community work. It is not, I believe, inevitable that, in every instance, all of community psychology will capitulate to the demands of capital. However, the embeddedness of most community psychology within neoliberal institutions should not be ignored if, indeed, we are to develop an honest portrayal of the anti-capitalist capacities of community psychology and its adjacent practices (including a psychology of community).

Although the twinned histories of psychology and capitalism have received increasing study in recent years, community psychology's entwinement with neoliberalism has received less attention (see Canham et al., 2021; Fryer & Fox, 2015; Malherbe & Dlamini, 2020, for some exceptions). It would be incorrect to decry all of community psychology as wedded to or invested in the neoliberal order. Certainly, many of the critical variants of community psychology that emerged all over the world in the 1970s were explicitly anti-capitalist (see Fryer, 2008). There have always been community psychologists who have sought to resist the neoliberal status quo and assist community activists in creating the conditions that foster anti-capitalism (see Ratele et al., 2018). Yet, for the most part, mainstream community psychologists have adhered to the neoliberal project's liberal-philanthropic paradigm, promoting distributive justice within the strictures of capital while refusing to declare their politics (Burton et al., 2012), thereby reproducing neoliberal rationality by default (Malherbe & Dlamini, 2020).

Although mainstream community psychology does not, in itself, constitute an ideology, it can be, and often is, used to advance neoliberalism's ideological mandate. Much community psychology assumes the rhetoric of social justice in order to legitimise itself within and for neoliberal ideology (Gokani & Walsh, 2017), creating "progressive identity spaces" that function as self-promotion devices for individual community psychologists (González Rey, 2016). Despite what its adherents claim, a community psychology of this sort can only but sanction politically conservative, top-down community development strategies which inadvertently reinforce systematic inequalities by ignoring individual agency (Coimbra et al., 2012; Fryer & Fox, 2015).

The inability of much of today's community psychology to go beyond the dictates of the neoliberal project seems to jar somewhat with the rhetoric surrounding its disciplinary origins. As a formalised discipline, community psychology emerged, in large part, as a reaction to the failures and perceived irrelevance of mainstream psychology and its focus on the individual at the expense of the individual-in-society (Angelique & Culley, 2007; Langhout, 2016). Yet, community psychology has, by and large, failed to go beyond the individualist purview of mainstream psychology, with concepts like "prevention" and "self-sufficiency" repeatedly evoked by community psychologists at a myopically individualist level (Orford, 2008). Hugo Canham and his colleagues (2021) argue that this failure to consider the collective is a result of mainstream community psychology's allegiance to capital. Gokani and Walsh (2017) demonstrate that the early iterations of "official" community psychology in the United States claimed inspiration from, rather than forged links with, different social justice movements of the day, with the activist role of community psychologists left as an "open question" (Langhout, 2016). In this regard, activism of any kind, let alone anti-capitalist action, was largely done away with by those practising mainstream community psychology. Class issues, Gokani and Walsh

(2017) insist, were especially absent in the early days of mainstream community psychology (see also Orford, 2008), with consumerist ideology oftentimes directly reflected within—rather than challenged by—those practising the discipline (Trickett, 2015).

Mainstream community psychology's adherence to capitalism is partly due to its weddedness to neoliberal institutions (Canham et al., 2021). It is because community psychology is housed in and supported by neoliberal institutions that community psychologists tend to enforce middle-class values and, in acting as agents of corporate power, seek out market or State-oriented solutions to social problems which are, themselves, products of the free market and the neoliberal State (see Fox, 2011). Clinical community psychologists, for instance, are usually driven by the same profit motives as the medical and psychiatric industries, with mental health divorced from its social context and turned into a commodity (Esposito & Perez, 2014). A community psychology that opposes the neoliberal system within which it is embedded is not only likely to lose funding, but may also be labelled violent, unethical, and/or unscientific (Ratele et al., 2018). As such, mainstream community psychology tends to be more concerned with its own identity (one that is to be bought, sold, and advertised in the marketplace) than with resisting capitalism (Malherbe & Dlamini, 2020).

Today, much mainstream community psychology aligns with the neoliberal political project by psychologising, de-politicising, and pathologising anti-capitalist movements (see de Oliveira & Júnior, 2022; Malherbe & Dlamini, 2020) all while claiming to mobilise them towards politically progressive ends (Walsh & Gokani, 2014). Community psychology of this kind tends to assist people in acclimatising to capitalism, improving their experience of it rather than working to dismantle it (Malherbe & Dlamini, 2020). We saw this in places like Brazil and England, where many community psychologists participated in psychologising—and consequentially neutering—the politics of grassroots resistance movements fighting imperialism and austerity (see de Oliveira & Júnior, 2022; Coimbra et al., 2012). This sort of adjustment-seeking individualism can also be observed in several mainstream community psychology interventions that are taking place in prisons, factories, hospitals, and schools (see Fox, 2011). The role that mainstream community psychology has played in better-integrating people into capitalist structures has moulded much of the discipline into an apparatus of neoliberal rationality.

Mainstream community psychology has also assisted in the production of neoliberal ideology through its conception of and approach to community. The contradictions inherent to any community tend to be brushed over—or understood as surpassable differences—by either valorising communities (constructing them as the epitome of consensus, democracy, and/or prospering in the face of adversity) or demonising them (establishing them as violent, Other, and/or pathological) (see Coimbra et al., 2012; Malherbe et al., 2021). An illusion of coherence is, therefore, established around the notion of "community" in order to bypass the historically contingent, multitudinous composition of a given community. Neoliberal multicultural ideology can then be encouraged because the "bad" and "good" communities which are said to exist side by side are made to seem like the result of intolerant attitudes. Similarly, regressive notions of diversity can be offered by community psychologists as surrogates for political struggle (Malherbe & Dlamini, 2020). These tired, irrelevant, and static theoretical models of community do little more than engender the so-called psy-complex (see Rose, 1985), that is, foster docility and self-management among knowable, productive, and rational communities (see Esposito & Perez, 2014; Ratner, 2019). When community psychology approaches the notion of community in these ways, community engagement itself becomes confined to a corporatised and transactional form whose principal function is to satisfy the neoliberal requirements of funders (de Oliveira & Júnior, 2022; Fourie & Terre Blanche, 2019). Resultantly, relatively little experimentation has occurred in mainstream community psychology with respect to fostering links and creating solidarities between and within dynamic, antagonistic communities (see Fox, 2011).

Knowledge-making within mainstream and even some critical variants of community psychology remains tied to neoliberal rationality (see Canham et al., 2021). The most influential community psychology journals are owned by corporations, with middle-class, Eurocentric values frequently taken as the ideological norm within these journals (Angelique & Culley, 2007). The English language, for instance, is typically understood as the gold standard within these journals. Moreover, the manner by which much community psychology is taught usually engages marginally, if at all, with issues of class and how class relates to racism, sexism, and disability within and across communities (Walsh & Gokani, 2014). In considering all of this, community psychology has involved itself not only in epistemic violence (i.e. harmful representational practices that cohere with neoliberal imperialism) but also in epistemicide, whereby the knowledges—as well as the knowledge-making resources and traditions—of othered peoples (knowledges which are not immediately marketable and are thus, according to neoliberal rationality, useless) are muted, eviscerated, and denied institutional support (see Malherbe et al., 2022, and Chap. 5). As such, Gokani and Walsh (2017) argue that mainstream community psychology has come to represent an "administrative science" (p. 291) that works in the service of neoliberalism's industrial, commercial, military, and criminal justice institutions.

Mainstream community psychology has, for the most part, been of little use to anti-capitalism. This is not to say that a neoliberalised mainstream community psychology has been altogether useless with respect to fighting for social justice. Indeed, community psychology of this kind is usually well-funded and can, therefore, contribute to some positive social change. Yet, such change can only ever occur within the logic, structures, and rationality of neoliberal capitalism, meaning that it is inherently constrained (Fourie & Terre Blanche, 2019). When community psychologists do consider the economy, it tends to be understood as a structural issue, rather than a site of intervention (Zlotowitz & Burton, 2022). It is thus under the guise of progressive rhetoric that most mainstream community psychology engagements bolster the neoliberal political project by reproducing—rather than seriously challenging—neoliberal rationality and ideology.

Conclusion

In this chapter, I have conceptualised neoliberalism in three ways: as a political project, an ideology, and a rationality. The point, I insist, is not to try to perceive neoliberalism as a coherent entity that reflects each of these conceptions at once. Instead, we can think of neoliberalism as a matrix in which each of these conceptions connects with the others in response to different events, crises, and actions (see Fine & Saad-Filho, 2017). Throughout its history, mainstream community psychology, I argue, has serviced neoliberalism in different ways and has, in turn, been rewarded by neoliberalism for this service. An anti-capitalist psychology of community must remain attentive to this history lest it unwittingly repeats it.

We should never attempt to understand neoliberal capitalism without its negation, that is, anti-capitalism (Latham, 2018). I use the term anti-capitalism rather than anti-neoliberalism because what must be resisted is not just the neoliberal particularities that have informed capitalism's most recent formation, but capitalism itself. When poor and working people are given concessions under capitalism, these are not the result of neoliberal benevolence, but a consequence of anti-capitalist action. Whether we consider neoliberalism as a political project, an ideology, or a normative rationality, it has always been met with resistance that shapes the forms that it is able to take. The crisis of legitimacy that neoliberalism has been facing since the global economic crash of 2008 and 2009 (a crisis that has been reiterated once again by the COVID-19 pandemic) has meant that capitalist powers are unable to command the consent they once did (Harvey, 2020). Today's capitalism has begun to lose control of its contradictions (see Amin, 2014b), with anti-capitalism fermenting all over the world: in the streets as well as at the points of production, realisation, and social reproduction (Fraser et al., 2019). It is to this ferment that an anti-capitalist psychology of community must be of use.

References

Ailon, G. (2022). Profit, self, and agency: A reevaluation. *Critical Sociology, 48*(2), 251–264.

Amin, S. (1989). *Eurocentrism*. Zed Books.

Amin, S. (2010). *The law of worldwide value*. Monthly Review Press.

Amin, S. (2014a). *Capitalism in the age of globalization–The management of contemporary society*. Zed Books.

Amin, S. (2014b). *The implosion of capitalism*. Pluto Press.

Angelique, H. L., & Culley, M. R. (2007). History and theory of community psychology: An international perspective of community psychology in the United States: Returning to political, critical and ecological roots. In S. M. Reich, M. Riemer, I. Prilleltensky, & M. Montero (Eds.), *International community psychology: History and theories (pp. 37–62)*. Springer.

Boas, T. C., & Gans-Morse, J. (2009). Neoliberalism: From new liberal philosophy to anti-liberal slogan. *Studies in Comparative International Development, 44*(2), 137–161.

Brown, W. (2006). *Regulating aversion: Tolerance in the age of identity and empire*. Princeton University Press.

Brown, W. (2015). *Undoing the demos: Neoliberalism's stealth revolution*. Zone Books.

Brown, W. (2019). *In the ruins of neoliberalism: The rise of antidemocratic politics in the west.* Columbia University Press.

Burton, M., Kagan, C., & Duckett, P. (2012). Making the psychological political–challenges for community psychology. *Global Journal of Community Psychology Practice, 3,* 1–11.

Canham, H., Bowman, B., Graham, T., Stevens, G., Langa, M., Jithoo, V., & Alexander, D. (2021). Conundrums in teaching decolonial critical community psychology within the context of neo-liberal market pressures. *Journal of Social Issues.* Advance online publication https://doi.org/10.1111/josi.12462.

Césaire, A. (1972). *Discourse on colonialism.* Monthly Review Press.

Chibber, V. (2022). *The class matrix: Social theory after the cultural turn.* Harvard University Press.

Coimbra, J. L., Duckett, P., Fryer, D., Makkawi, I., Menezes, I., Seedat, M., & Walker, C. (2012). Rethinking community psychology: Critical insights. *The Australian Community Psychologist, 24,* 135–142.

de Oliveira, I. F., & Júnior, F. L. (2022). Contributions of Marxism to community psychology: Emancipation in debate. In C. Kagan, J. Akhurst, J. Alfaro, R. Lawthom, M. Richards, & A. Zambrano (Eds.), *The Routledge international handbook of community psychology: Facing global crises with hope (pp. 32–45).* Routledge.

Eagleton, T. (1991). *Ideology: An introduction.* Verso.

Esposito, L., & Perez, F. M. (2014). Neoliberalism and the commodification of mental health. *Humanity and Society, 38*(4), 414–442.

Fanon, F. (1963). *The wretched of the earth.* Grove Press.

Fanon, F. (1967). *Black skin, white masks.* Grove Press.

Federici, S. (2004). *Caliban and the witch: Women, the body and primitive accumulation.* Autonomedia.

Fine, B., & Saad-Filho, A. (2017). Thirteen things you need to know about neoliberalism. *Critical Sociology, 43*(4–5), 685–706.

Foucault, M. (2010). *The birth of biopolitics: Lectures at the Collège de France, 1978–1979.* Picador.

Fourie, E., & Terre Blanche, M. (2019). About accountants and translators: Reshaping community engagement in South African psychology. *South Africa Journal of Psychology, 49*(1), 39–51.

Fox, D. (2011). Anarchism and psychology. *Theory in Action, 4*(4), 31–48.

Fraser, N. (2014). Behind Marx's hidden abode. *New Left Review, 85*(2), 55–74.

Fraser, N., Arruzza, C., & Bhattacharya, T. (2019). *Feminism for the 99 percent: A manifesto.* Verso.

Fromm, E. (1942). *Fear of freedom.* Routledge.

Fryer, D. (2008). Some questions about "the history of community psychology". *Journal of Community Psychology, 36*(5), 572–586.

Fryer, D., & Fox, R. (2015). Community psychology: Subjectivity, power, collectivity. In I. Parker (Ed.), *Handbook of critical psychology (pp. 145–154).* Routledge.

Galtung, J. (1969). Violence, peace, and peace research. *Journal of Peace Research, 6*(3), 167–191.

Ghosh, J. (2021). Interpreting contemporary imperialism: Lessons from Samir Amin. *Review of African Political Economy, 48*(167), 8–14.

Glynos, J. (2001). The grip of ideology: A Lacanian approach to the theory of ideology. *Journal of Political Ideologies, 6*(2), 191–214.

Gokani, R., & Walsh, R. T. (2017). On the historical and conceptual foundations of a community psychology of social transformation. *American Journal of Community Psychology, 59*(3–4), 284–294.

González Rey, F. (2016). Paths, development and discontinuity of some critical approaches to psychology in Latin America: What happened in that history? *Annual Review of Critical Psychology, 10,* 642–662.

Gramsci, A. (1971). *Selections from the prison notebooks.* Lawrence & Wishart.

Han, B. (2017). *Psychopolitics: Neoliberalism and new technologies of power.* Verso.

Hardt, M., & Negri, A. (2009). *Commonwealth.* Harvard University Press.

Harvey, D. (2005). *A brief history of neoliberalism.* Oxford University Press.

Harvey, D. (2017). *The ways of the world*. Profile Books.

Harvey, D. (2020). *The anti-capitalist chronicles*. Pluto Press.

Hobsbawm, E. (1994). *The age of extremes: 1914–1991*. Michael Joseph.

Holloway, J. (2010). *Crack capitalism*. Pluto Press.

Kotsko, A. (2018). *Neoliberalism's demons: On the political theology of late capital*. Stanford University Press.

Langhout, R. D. (2016). This is not a history lesson; this is agitation: A call for a methodology of diffraction in US-based community psychology. *American Journal of Community Psychology, 58*(3–4), 322–328.

Latham, R. (2018). Contemporary capitalism, uneven development, and the arc of anti-capitalism. *Global Discourse, 8*(2), 169–186.

Maldonado-Torres, N. (2007). On the coloniality of being: Contributions to the development of a concept. *Cultural Studies, 21*(2–3), 240–270.

Malherbe, N. (2018). Expanding conceptions of liberation: Holding Marxisms with liberation psychology. *Theory & Psychology, 28*(3), 340–357.

Malherbe, N. (2020). Articulating liberation psychologies of culture. *Journal of Theoretical and Philosophical Psychology, 40*(4), 203–218.

Malherbe, N. (2021a). A psychopolitical interpretation of de-alienation: Marxism, psychoanalysis, and liberation psychology. *Psychoanalysis, Culture & Society, 26*(3), 263–283.

Malherbe, N. (2021b). De-ideologization, liberation psychology, and the place of contradiction. *Journal for the Theory of Social Behaviour*. Advance online publication. https://doi.org/10.1111/jtsb.12322.

Malherbe, N., & Dlamini, S. (2020). Troubling history and diversity: Disciplinary decadence in community psychology. *Community Psychology in Global Perspective, 6*(2/1), 144–157.

Malherbe, N., Seedat, M., & Suffla, S. (2021). Analyzing discursive constructions of community in newspaper articles. *American Journal of Community Psychology, 67*(3–4), 433–446.

Malherbe, N., Suffla, S., & Seedat, M. (2022). Epistemicide and epistemic freedom: Reflections for a decolonising community psychology. In C. Kagan, J. Akhurst, J. Alfaro, R. Lawthom, M. Richards, & A. Zambrano (Eds.), *The Routledge international handbook of community psychology: Facing global crises with hope (pp. 17–31)*. Routledge.

Mandel, E. (1979). *Late capitalism*. New Left Books.

Marx, K. (1977). *Capital: A critique of political economy* (Vol. 1). Vintage.

Marx, K., & Engels, F. (1970). *The German ideology*. International Publishers.

Mbembe, A. (2019). *Necropolitics*. Wits University Press.

McGowan, T. (2019). *Emancipation after Hegel: Achieving a contradictory revolution*. Columbia University Press.

Ndlovu-Gatsheni, S. J. (2021). Revisiting Marxism and decolonisation through the legacy of Samir Amin. *Review of African Political Economy, 48*(167), 50–65.

Ngwane, T. (2021). *Amakomiti: Grassroots democracy in South African shack settlements*. Pluto Press.

Nkrumah, K. (1965). *Neo-colonialism: The last stage of imperialism*. Thomas Nel.

Orford, J. (2008). *Community psychology: Challenges, controversies and emerging consensus*. John Wiley & Sons.

Patel, R., & Moore, J. W. (2018). *A history of the world in seven cheap things*. Verso.

Peck, J. (2001). Neoliberalizing states: Thin policies/hard outcomes. *Progress in Human Geography, 25*, 445–455.

Phelps, J. M., & White, C. M. (2018). Social psychology and neoliberalism: A critical commentary on McDonald, Gough, wearing, and Deville (2017). *Journal for the Theory of Social Behaviour, 48*(3), 390–396.

Ratele, K., Cornell, J., Dlamini, S., Helman, R., Malherbe, N., & Titi, N. (2018). Some basic questions about (a) decolonizing Africa(n)-centred psychology considered. *South Africa Journal of Psychology, 48*(3), 331–342.

Ratner, C. (2019). *Neoliberal psychology*. Springer.

Rodney, W. (1972). *How Europe underdeveloped Africa*. Bogle-L'Ouverture Publications.

Rose, N. (1985). Unreasonable rights: Mental illness and the limits of the law. *Journal of Law and Society, 12*(2), 199–218.

Saad-Filho, A. (2017). Neoliberalism. In D. Brennan, D. Kristjanson-Gural, C. Mulder, & K. Olsen (Eds.), *Routledge handbook of Marxian economics (pp. 245–254)*. Routledge.

Shalhoub-Kevorkian, N., & Wahab, S. (2021). Colonial necrocapitalism, state secrecy and the Palestinian freedom tunnel. *Social and Health Sciences, 19*(2), 1–18.

Springer, S. (2012). Neoliberalism as discourse: Between Foucauldian political economy and Marxian poststructuralism. *Critical Discourse Studies, 9*(2), 133–147.

Steger, M., & Roy, R. (2021). *Neoliberalism: A very short introduction*. Oxford University Press.

Teo, T. (2018). Homo neoliberalus: From personality to forms of subjectivity. *Theory & Psychology, 28*(5), 581–599.

Therborn, G. (1980). *The ideology of power and the power of ideology*. Verso.

Trickett, E. J. (2015). Seymour Sarason remembered: "Plus ça change…", "psychology misdirected", and "community psychology and the anarchist insight". *American Journal of Community Psychology, 56*(3–4), 197–204.

Walsh, R. T., & Gokani, R. (2014). The personal and political economy of psychologists' desires for social justice. *Journal of Theoretical and Philosophical Psychology, 34*, 41–55.

Wark, M. (2017). *General intellects: Twenty-five thinkers for the twenty-first century*. Verso.

Wolff, R. P., Moore, B., & Marcuse, H. (1965). *A critique of pure tolerance*. Beacon Press.

Wright, E. O. (2015). *Understanding class*. Verso.

Wright, E. O. (2019). *How to be an anti-capitalist in the 21st century*. Verso.

Yeros, P., & Jha, P. (2020). Late neo-colonialism: Monopoly capitalism in permanent crisis. *Agrarian South: Journal of Political Economy, 9*(1), 78–93.

Žižek, S. (1989). *The sublime object of ideology*. Verso.

Žižek, S. (2020). *A left that dares to speak its name: 34 untimely interventions*. Polity.

Zlotowitz, S., & Burton, M. H. (2022). Community psychology and political economy. In C. Kagan, J. Akhurst, J. Alfaro, R. Lawthom, M. Richards, & A. Zambrano (Eds.), *The Routledge international handbook of community psychology: Facing global crises with hope (pp. 46–59)*. Routledge.

.

Chapter 3
Resisting the Capitalist Political Project

The neoliberal political project, as recounted in Chap. 2, is near-omnipotent in its globalised, neocolonial purview. Yet, as we are seeing all over the world today, the expansiveness of neoliberalism also means that it can be resisted in many ways. Resisting the capitalist political project depends on the actions of people who, together, make use of stage-oriented strategies and tactics to apply pressure to the reproduction and realisation of capital (Amin, 2014; Harvey, 2020). Coordinating such action is, however, tremendously difficult. It carries with it much affect and tension, and it requires people to look inwards and outwards while learning from—rather than becoming paralysed by—political failures and setbacks. In this chapter, I am concerned with these kinds of psychopolitical questions which characterise collective resistance to the capitalist political project. As such, I consider how we might put a psychology of community to work for anti-capitalist social movements (i.e. formalised anti-capitalist politics) which—as Erik Olin Wright (2019) explains—resist the capitalist project by struggling outside of State apparatuses in ways that do not attempt to gain State power. Specifically, I focus on the four modes of collective anti-capitalist resistance with which I have had the most experience in my community-engaged psychological work, namely, political organising, affective community-building, solidarity-making, and reflexive engagement.

I hope to make it clear that although an anti-capitalist psychology of community does not contain fixed content and will not find expression through a particular form, such a psychology must always contort and bend in accordance with the demands of anti-capitalist community struggles. At the same time, psychologists of community can work with activists to challenge potential and existing regressive elements within their movements. It would be imprudent to attribute any kind of revolutionary potential to psychology, but there is, I believe, a role that psychologists of community can play in some of the emotional and practical work involved in building and consolidating anti-capitalist movements.

Political Organising

Wright (2015) insists that in addition to resisting the reproduction of the capitalist political economy, "the balance of power also needs to be changed. And since this shift in the balance of power will be costly to those in privileged positions, it will

© The Author(s), under exclusive license to Springer Nature Switzerland AG 2022
N. Malherbe, *For an Anti-capitalist Psychology of Community*, Community
Psychology, https://doi.org/10.1007/978-3-030-99696-3_3

only occur through a process of mobilization and struggle" (p. 184). It is, therefore, heartening that we are seeing, all over the world today, a surge of anti-capitalist mobilisation. Some of this mobilisation activity is planned, while some of it has been spontaneous (see Ngwane, 2021). Yet, as encouraging and inspiring as this might be, mobilisation does not necessarily lead to political organisation. In other words, collective mobilisation against the neoliberal project rarely assumes a sustainable formation. Although a protest in one part of the world can strengthen a (potentially globalised) network of anti-capitalist protest movements, broad-based anti-capitalist resistance to the neoliberal project remains fragmented (Harvey, 2020). Without sustained political organising, these anti-capitalist moments, insurgent as they are, are unlikely to become organised movements that can take power and offer systems-focused solutions to dehumanising neoliberal policies, debt peonage, neocolonial extractivism, and financialisation (see Harvey, 2017; Malherbe, 2020; Ndlovu-Gatsheni, 2021).

Within community settings, political organising is crucial for ensuring that anti-capitalist resistance efforts are sustainable, appealing, committed to a common set of goals, oriented towards workable strategies, resourced, and compelled by a collectively articulated political agenda (see Minkler, 2012). It is in these ways that community-based political organising strives to move from abstractions to materialising political goals. Yet, political organising is tremendously challenging psychological work. The continued stress on the imperative to organise politically can, at times, ignore the psychological turmoil and mental demands that can characterise organising (Fox, 2011). It is also difficult to appeal anti-capitalist movements to masses of people (Žižek, 2020), especially in contexts where neoliberal forces are working to actively break these movements (Ratner, 2019). Movements, themselves, are often mired in internal and external squabbles, and individualism remains rampant. Additionally, currents of oppression (e.g. racism, sexism, ableism, xenophobia) oftentimes infiltrate and fracture anti-capitalist movements from within. For many, struggle contexts contain elements of trauma which mirror the oppressively racialised and gendered nature of neoliberalism (Malherbe, 2021a). All of this can result in what Laurence Cox (2011) refers to as "activist burnout", a psychological phenomenon that has been largely—and shamefully—neglected by psychology (and even when psychologists do pay attention to activist burnout, they tend to disavow any explicitly political commitment; see Sloan & Brush, 2022). None of what I have raised here is to argue against political organising. On the contrary, it is to stress the imperative for diverse forms of organising that speak to the contradictions that mark activist subjects and the capitalist society that they seek to change (Amin, 2014). To be sustainable, appealing, and useful, organising must remain attentive to the psychological inasmuch as the political.

When considering capitalism as a political project, an anti-capitalist psychology of community strives to be a psychology *for* rather than *on* movement activism (see Sloan & Brush, 2022). Therefore, an anti-capitalist psychology of community does not merely study the emotional facets of political organising from a cool distance (as is the wont of most "politicised" psychology; see Malherbe, 2021b). Rather, such a psychology necessitates working with people's emotions to assist them in organising against capitalism more effectively. This is tricky because we are repeatedly made to feel good—and told that we are psychologically healthy—when we comply with the profit-enhancing dictates of the neoliberal project (Han, 2017). The point, then, for psychologists working with political organisers is to strike a balance between critically interrogating comrades' feelings while also trusting what it is that feelings can tell us about anti-capitalist organising (e.g. what is politically effective and what is not). Put differently, psychologists of community and those with whom they work should remain aware of how neoliberalism mobilises their feelings—both positively and negatively—while, simultaneously, engaging these same feelings insofar as they facilitate modes of action and solidarity that reflect a movement's broader political agenda (see Teo, 2018a). Angelique Harris (2018) notes that gendered, racial, class-based, and sexual oppression lies at the root of the anger that many Black women organisers experience, and it is this anger that drives their activism and ensures that such activism informs their sense of identity. As Gwen Carr, the mother of Eric Garner,[1] proclaimed in the aftermath of her son's death: "I had to change my mourning into a movement, my pain into purpose, and sorrow into a strategy" (Latif & Latif, 2016, paragraph 36). Her feelings became the impetus for organising. In another example, Oyakawa et al. (2021) found that when community organisers confronted painful feelings and vulnerabilities, they were better able to take on some of the stressors that political organising entails. In each of these examples, the neoliberalisation of feelings is resisted so that feelings can serve as the impetus for acting against the neoliberal project. If psychologists of community wish to be of assistance to political organising—to use psychology *for* social movements—they can act against the foundations of their discipline by working with collectives to politicise, rather than psychologise, their feelings. As such, psychologists of community are urged to take up Byung-Chul Han's (2017) call to *de-psychologise*, which entails disinvesting from the ways that neoliberalism (often with the help of psychologists) draws on emotion to offer static, quantifiable images of the self, and instead move towards an action-oriented approach to emotion that is attuned to what emotions tell us about organising. It is through a process of de-psychologisation that psychologists of community can work with anti-capitalist organisers to harness the actional potential of emotion, as well as recognise and attend to the emotional toll that anti-capitalist organising can take.

For much community psychology, conflict has been understood as an issue that is to be resolved, with little engagement with the generative qualities of conflict (Brodsky & Faryal, 2006; Nelson & Prilleltensky, 2010). This drive for resolution risks not only ignoring the material circumstances that give rise to conflict in the first place (see Cornell et al., 2020) but also promoting adaptation to capitalism over anti-capitalist antagonism. Psychologists of community can work with activists to engage conflict in accordance with their movement's anti-capitalist politics, reassessing these politics in light of this conflict. In this, political organising strives to hold, rather than resolve, conflict in ways that strengthen people's attachment to a

---

[1] An unarmed African American man who was murdered by police officers in New York City for selling loose cigarettes

particular anti-capitalist politics. Although this work is difficult, unpleasant, and often very tense, it is essential for strengthening people's political commitments and their ability to work together to action these commitments. Tensions, failures of connection, and conflict can all become the basis for new egalitarian and democratic relations, conditions, values, and principles within movements (Ratner, 2019). By embracing conflict, psychologists of community working for anti-capitalist organising can retool conflict so that it reflects what Harrell and Bond (2006) call connected disruption, wherein conflict strengthens solidarities by exploring avenues of cohesiveness through disunity (see Cornell et al., 2020). As Robert Latham (2018) notes, this sort of Marxian dialectical negation, or ethic of discomfort (see Malherbe & Dlamini, 2020), is useful for ensuring that movements are open to revising and reforming their political commitments, strategies, and tactics. The point, then, is not to become debilitated, politically paralysed, and fearful of perpetual conflict, but to use conflict as a point of tension that is necessary for the kinds of growth and adaptability upon which the sustainability and livelihood of any anti-capitalist movement depend (see Malherbe & Dlamini, 2020).

Although the difficult emotional work involved in political organising should not be overlooked, psychologists of community should not brush over the joyful kinds of affect that can accompany organising. For instance, Kevin Carriere (2020) has demonstrated that organised labour can foster within comrades feelings of connectedness, autonomy, trust, fellowship, a sense of community, higher life satisfaction, and increased self-esteem. In their work, Hardt and Negri (2009) are especially partial to discussing the moments of joy and even love that occur when people organise against capitalism (see also Malherbe, 2021b). Jodi Dean (2019) similarly speaks of the elation that one feels when forming bonds with comrades, bonds which are repeatedly discouraged by the neoliberal order (see also Ratner, 2019). An awareness of the positive feelings generated within struggle can assist psychologists of community in working with people to activate the healing potential of activist spaces and the modes of empathetic connection and association that such spaces can allow. Collective healing of this sort may then become a demand of anti-capitalist movements, which is especially important in contexts where intergenerational trauma remains unacknowledged (Malherbe, 2021b). Psychologists of community who are inattentive to the positive feelings that accompany anti-capitalist struggle are, therefore, disregarding a useful means of broadening the appeal of this struggle.

Raymond Williams' (1977) conception of a structure of feeling denotes the ways by which meanings and values are lived, felt, and made into habit, intuition, and sensibility. Although structures of feeling are said to characterise particular cultural epochs, they are not always easy to articulate and sometimes—because they exist beyond our symbolic order—resist enunciation altogether (see also Malherbe, 2021a). Yet, one's inability or difficulty to articulate a structure of feeling has important implications for political organising precisely because a specific structure of feeling can point towards political desires that are not within the immediate confines of capitalist symbolisation (see Williams, 1977). We cannot speak an anti-capitalist structure of feeling because the language of capitalism does not allow us to.

Psychologists of community can work with activists to better speak structures of feeling within their movements and to flesh out what these structures of feeling mean for the kinds of changes that people want to see in their communities and how they want these changes enacted. As such, activists can communicate (or perhaps, rather, approach an articulation of) those political demands and desires that do not always have a language available to them. Psychological work of this kind enables us to take seriously the symbolic, the affective, and the pragmatic within organisational spaces (Malherbe, 2020).

Although an anti-capitalist psychology of community is well-suited to working with the emotional dimensions of political organising (e.g. through communication strategies and holding group affect; see Long, 2021), we should not discount the usefulness of such a psychology when it comes to the pragmatic elements of political organising. This is especially so in cases where psychologists of community draw on institutional resources to assist political organisers. Resources of this kind may include funding, transportation, and the use of venues, all of which are essential for organising (see Malherbe & Dlamini, 2020). As such, psychologists of community can deploy their institutional embeddedness in strategic ways that allow them to go beyond psychology's narrow disciplinary dictates and expectations (see also Chap. 1).

Political organising is central to the development of a critical consciousness that drives people to not only challenge capitalists but overthrow capitalist institutions and liberate themselves (Hannah, 2021). An anti-capitalist psychology of community should not shy away from the immensely difficult emotional work involved in political organising. Moreover, whenever possible, psychologists of community should attempt to unconditionally avail the materials necessary for undertaking this notoriously under-resourced work. Rejecting the role of leader or expert, psychologists of community can work with anti-capitalist activists and organisers to symbolise their feelings and address internal conflicts in ways that strengthen—rather than fracture—political commitments (altering these commitments if need be). In this, an anti-capitalist psychology of community takes seriously both the affective and the material dimensions of movement organising.

Solidarity-Making

Solidarity has become something of a buzzword. It is frequently used rhetorically or to signal one's awareness of injustice. We cannot allow solidarity to sink to such depths. We must "take back the word" (Hardt & Negri, 2017) by refusing any attempt to debase the political radicality of solidarity. In seeking to retain solidarity's anti-capitalist character, David Featherstone (2012) has defined it, quite simply, as the transformative and relational bonds—forged in the context of political struggle—which are required to build political commitment. As has already been mentioned, building anti-capitalist power is immensely challenging (if also, at times, exhilarating, thrilling, and joyful) within a neoliberal context that encourages and incentivises competitive individualism (see Ratner, 2019; Žižek, 2020). Indeed, the isolated "lonely crowds" produced under capitalism tend to disguise the unity of poverty, creating either societies devoid of community (Debord, 1977) or communities that are geographically removed from broader society (Mbembe, 2021). Moreover, when located in neoliberal political structures, well-meaning efforts to build solidarity are repeatedly replaced with humanitarian projects and aid programmes that are determined by capital (Ndlovu-Gatsheni, 2021). We see this in the philanthropic approach—which seems to have little concern with anti-capitalist solidarity—that is assumed by much mainstream community psychology (Burton et al., 2012).

Wright (2019) considers community and solidarity as operating together, as a piece. He writes that "Community/solidarity expresses the principle that people ought to cooperate with each other not simply because of what they receive, but also from a real commitment to the well-being of others and a sense of moral obligation that it is right to do" (Wright, 2019, p. 18). However, anti-capitalist community work requires psychologists to go beyond Wright's optimism. As Bettez and Hytten (2013) argue, communities are defined as much by those who they exclude as they are by those who they include. What, we might ask, do these inclusions and exclusions mean for solidarity-building across and within antagonistic communities; solidarity-building among those who are not yet convinced by anti-capitalist politics; and solidarity-building across different identities? These questions, which seem to orbit around issues of identity and identification, are psychological inasmuch as they are social and political and are thus of concern to an anti-capitalist psychology of community.

Solidarity is premised on expansion. In what Harvey (2017)—who is, here, recalling Williams (2016)—refers to as militant particularism, a set of struggles at the local level can be drawn on and used as a model for creating solidarity and connecting with other, global, struggles. This is, of course, tremendously difficult work, with cultural and even economic particularities at the local level rarely mapping neatly onto other contexts. Moreover, as Williams (2016) notes, translating political loyalties from the local to the global is immensely challenging and involves considerable tensions which typically go unresolved. Anti-capitalist linkages between the Global North and Global South, although crucial for defeating imperialist monopoly (which has been cemented since the breakdown of the Bretton Woods Agreement in the 1970s; see Chap. 2), are disincentivised via racist discourse and the ways by which Global North workers are, oftentimes, compensated in better ways than those in the South (Yeros & Jha, 2020). Instating militant particularism is, however, not impossible, and although globalisation has seen the worldwide dominance of capital, it also provides people with opportunities to create solidarity and identify how the world is common, connected, and shared (Hardt & Negri, 2009). In fact, we see global solidarities in action all the time. For instance, when it was revealed that police in Ferguson, Missouri, were firing onto anti-racist protesters the same kind of teargas that Israeli authorities were firing onto Palestinian activists, these activists in Palestine offered advice to the anti-racist protesters in the United States on how to effectively treat this teargas (Davis, 2016). Psychologists of community should similarly strive to assist in globalising solidarity in whatever ways they can. This might involve drawing on institutional resources (e.g. computers, Internet, printing) to assist activists from around the world in fostering connections or even to draw on the global network of critical, anti-capitalist psychologists to share politically engaged mental health practices, discuss how psychology has been effective in different settings, and debate when one's role as a psychologist should be rescinded and the role of citizen activist taken up (see Malherbe, Ratele, et al., 2021a). It is in these ways that psychologists of community can work to build anti-capitalism through the militant particular, which is to say, a pluriversal global solidarity premised on connecting different struggles for the purpose of creating a common humanity.

Psychologists can, however, also assist in building solidarities at the level of community. Elsewhere (see Malherbe, 2021b), I have described how psychologists of community can work with activists to establish what Laclau and Mouffe (1985) refer to as a chain of equivalence, where different social movements articulate their political demands to and for one another in an effort to establish anti-capitalist coalitions. Although articulation of this kind can take many forms, I argue that psychologists of community can use emotionality to create visceral chains of equivalence that can enhance how activists connect with one another. Fostering psychic bonds in this way enables psychologists of community to work with activists to strengthen the political bonds on which solidarity depends. Bonds of this sort are crucial for bringing about an awareness of how the struggles of another, under capitalism's mutualist society, are always also one's own struggles (see Davis, 2016). The fight against anti-Semitism and the fight for Palestinian rights are, for example, part of the same anti-capitalist struggle (Žižek, 2020), just as the fight for land and the fight against police brutality in South Africa constitute a common resistance to the post-apartheid State's embrace of the neoliberal project (Ngwane, 2021). Although struggles such as these might appear disparate, situating them as anti-capitalist can allow for an entry point into cooperation and solidarity-building (see Fraser, 2014). This realm of interconnected struggles thereby attempts to address the capitalist project's totality (Harvey, 2020). Psychologists of community can work across different struggles to build solidarity via empathetic intersubjective connections (e.g. with storytelling and narrative group therapy) and in this strive to prevent the foreclosure of the capitalist totality. Although these connections are often fraught, they nonetheless hold the potential to unmask how struggles are only artificially segregated under capitalism (Malherbe, 2020).

While identity-based movements face considerable hostility within the neoliberal project (especially in those countries experiencing fascist and neo-fascist onslaughts), it is less often acknowledged that these movements also face discrimination and dismissal by parts of the political Left. Orthodox Marxists are often vehemently opposed to questions of identity, arguing that despite the material rootedness of identities, identity as such divides the working class along arbitrary lines. Yet, identities—socially constructed as they are—have real consequences that are both psychic and material and thus contain within them important considerations for solidarity-making. In Chap. 2, I touched on some of these consequences, including the gendered and racialised divisions of labour. Although solidarity-building rests, ultimately, on a commitment to a particular politics (an anti-capitalist politics, in our case), one's identity plays an important role in connecting with politics. A political commitment, after all, usually means that politics are made part of one's identity. Identity-based movements can, and frequently do, ensure that anti-capitalist movements remain inclusive and that they do not reinscribe oppressive patterns of power (e.g. sexism, racism, xenophobia, ableism) that mimic neoliberal logic and weaken the solidarity relation. Many of history's most effective anti-capitalist movements were highly cognisant of identity. Some of the clearest examples here are noted in the decolonial movements of the twentieth century; however, there are plenty of others. Featherstone (2012), for instance, recounts how, historically, women-led trade unions were instrumental in addressing patriarchal currents that run through many (implicitly, male-dominated) labour unions. We also saw this in how transgender activists fought patriarchal currents within 2015's student movement in South Africa (Ndelu et al., 2017). Yet, these examples also point to an understandable reluctance on the part of many identity-based movements to form solidarities with others on the anti-capitalist Left. There is a risk of discrimination and even violence when attempting to form solidarities of this kind (Wilkinson, 2017).

Psychologists of community who work with activists to build solidarity across movements cannot presume an equal playing field on the basis of a shared anti-capitalist commitment. Doing so risks instating what Jo Freeman (1972), in a different context, called the tyranny of structurelessness, whereby a supposed absence of hierarchy allows oppressive power to operate under the guide of egalitarianism and therefore functions all the more effectively. Psychologists of community should work with activists and organisers within and across movements to acknowledge the unequal flows of power that define the solidarity relation if, indeed, these relations are to be built in a manner that is meaningful and that people are willing to sustain (see Sloan & Brush, 2022). As such, a broad-based anti-capitalist coalition may, paradoxically, depend on identity-based movements organising among themselves to articulate the conditions on which they will enter into the solidarity relation with other movements. Psychologists of community can assist with the articulation and communication of these conditions so long as activists permit them to do so. The stories and testimonials of individual activists, some of which are likely to be traumatic and/or affect-laden, can be important for fleshing out what it is that movements or groups require to begin building solidarity with others. The goal here is not, of course, to develop feelings of unconditional fondness for those with whom one struggles in solidarity, but to delineate the conditions of accountability on which meaningful solidarity depends (see Malherbe, 2021b). In this, organising separately against capitalist oppression can enable different collectives to eventually work with one another to strike, in solidarity, at capitalism as a political system (Hannah, 2021).

Attention to and sensitivity towards the role of identity within processes of solidarity-making should not mean that psychologists of community and activists engage identity without a critical eye. As the psychoanalysts remind us, identity does not avail psychic fullness—it misses, or fails to capture, those parts of the self that do not cohere with what it means to be identified as a particular subject (see Malherbe,

2021a). Under capitalism, people oftentimes develop an attachment to an identity that resembles the fetishistic attachment to property (Hardt & Negri, 2009). In the context of solidarity-making, psychologists of community should remain attuned to the psychic lack inherent to identity, not only because such lack drives how we identify and desire more generally (the appeal of fascist discourse, for instance, relies on its promise to fill subjective lack by eliminating the Other) but also because lack is, itself, conducive to psychosocial solidarity-making. While we cannot *know* the Other, we also cannot know ourselves entirely, and this mutual lacking can serve as a basis for establishing political connections not through a common identity (which comrades do not always have), but in relation to fighting a shared oppression that manifests differently for differently identifying people (Dean, 2019). Psychologists of community can, therefore, work with activists to build psychopolitical solidarity through a common (but differently constituted) mode of subjective lack (Malherbe, 2021a). Using lack to build solidarity rejects the moralistic notion of pure identity or subjectivity, whereby a virtuous, irreproachable self and/or Other works only to mask unequal relations of power and/or engender a patronising mode of engagement. Through lack, people can act democratically and desire in common with one another while still retaining their individual differences (Hardt & Negri, 2004). As Negri (2008) puts it, solidarity is "the articulation of subjectivity within the common ... [It is not] a machine for the flattening out of differences. On the contrary, it is open to singularities that live and produce within this common network" (p. 20). Solidarity of this sort rests on committing to a common anti-capitalist project while also accommodating the various ways by which the multitude relates to this project.

Solidarity-making faces tremendous challenges, such as overcoming privatised lives, the complex and fragmented class structures in which we all live, divisive racist and sexist discourse, and competition for resources (Wright, 2019). Yet, solidarity remains essential if we are to sustain political action and build the kinds of popular power from below which are necessary to combat the neoliberal political project. Our individual freedoms are always tied in with the progress of the collective, even when different struggles are made to appear separate from one another (Harvey, 2017). The role of the psychologist working with communities to build solidarity is one that concerns the building of political bonds through the knowledge that although the immediate benefits of the individual may diminish when one aligns with anti-capitalist struggle, the capacities of the collective are strengthened (Dean, 2019). These bonds, Erich Fromm (1942) contends, serve as the "one possible, productive solution" (p. 29) for combatting capitalism's individualism and divisiveness. It is only through active solidarity with others, Fromm (1942) argues, that one can access the self, the world, and others as a free and independent individual.

Affective Community-Building

Although a somewhat nebulous term, community-building refers to a process whereby members of a community mobilise around a common, pluriversal, sense of community in order to strengthen their collective capacity to address a set of community problems (Mannarini & Salvatore, 2019). When communities work together, in this way, to create the binding substance with which they identify, there may be an ethical incentive to act, together, on behalf of the community (Walter & Hyde, 2012). Community-building is not uniform or inherently progressive (see Ahmed, 2015; Bettez, 2011). For some, community is "a fiction in whose name one is ready to kill and to be killed as needed" (Mbembe, 2021, p. 188). However, community-building can also foster meaningful kinds of connection which are crucial for solidifying anti-capitalist organising and solidarity-making. Anti-capitalist commitment can, therefore, result in the formation of a community whose connective properties are continually negotiated by its members. I wish to argue that an especially fruitful means of anti-capitalist community-building for a psychology of community (where community-building has received relatively little attention; see Lazarus et al., 2017) is known as affective community-building, whereby affective bonds (i.e. feelings created within and between bodies that make emotional connections and reactions possible, Ahmed, 2015) are relied on to create cohesion and solidarity among communities. It is because affect can be directed (see Wetherell, 2015) that it is able to intensify the collective's commitment to an anti-capitalist project. Although affective community-building stresses the importance of individual difference within the process of building community (Von Scheve, 2019), it differs from the kinds of emotion-oriented political organising discussed earlier because it is concerned with the notion of community—rather than formalised political movements per se—as well as affect (which is bodily and transferable, unlike emotion which is cognitive). Where working towards a set of political goals is the prerequisite for one's belonging to a particular anti-capitalist project (a belonging that can, certainly, be highly emotional), how people *feel together* in relation to this project signifies their affective belonging to an anti-capitalist community (see Mouffe, 2018).

Affective community-building can allow people to break from the stifling, top-down rationalist frameworks (which tend to align with the neoliberal project) that have been employed in mainstream community-building activity (Mouffe, 2018; Zink, 2019), much of which has been inspired by the pragmatism of Saul Alinsky's (1971) community organising methods. Indeed, when people rely on affect for anti-capitalist community-building, they can avoid slipping into corporate models of "measurable" participation which rely on immediate outcomes, market logic, and instrumentality (Fourie & Terre Blanche, 2019). Yet, at the same time, when psychologists of community and the activists with whom they work rely on affect to build anti-capitalist community bonds, they are likely to encounter several challenges that may not be as apparent within mainstream, instrumentalist community-building. For example, people might be discouraged and disappointed when they do not make community in the ways that they anticipated (Bettez & Hytten, 2013) or when community becomes a means for exclusion and fractioning rather than connection (Bettez, 2011). It is because affect works beyond linguistic scripts that it can hold the potential to be misread and/or interpreted in ways that can harm (see Ahmed, 2015), with affect, itself, not being immune to neoliberal instrumentality (Han, 2017). Moreover, sustaining affective bonds, and the difficult psychological processes and inward reflection that community-building entails, can hinder and debilitate the actioning of the political goals of community-building (Rowe & Royster, 2017). Nonetheless, affective community-building can assist those involved in an anti-capitalist psychology of community to foster connections from below as well as through the contradictory, ever-shifting nature of community (see Bettez, 2011) and in this reject the hierarchical currents inherent to Alinsky's (1971) influential community-building model. Mainstream community-building can, and often does, risk relegating issues of community to a single, homogenised voice, whereby affective community-building harnesses the complex and multiple sets of overlapping boundaries that constitute all communities, engaging these beyond singular or fixed parameters that fetishise "the local". Community connectedness is, therefore, not imposed by community outsiders, as is the case with much mainstream psychology as well as Alinsky's (1971) methods. Instead, a community's emotional resources and affective interactional capacities are relied upon to unite bodies and minds around an anti-capitalist politics. As such, through affective community-building, community constitutes a mode of becoming (Bettez & Hytten, 2013) that is always democratically negotiated by the feeling collective, rather than a fixed abstraction removed from people's material concerns (Williams, 2016).

The process of affective community-building can form the basis of what are referred to as affective communities, that is, the temporal, spontaneous, and generative solidarities that bind affected and affecting bodies and which give rise to intense and immersive forms of integration and belonging (see Zink, 2019). Affective communities can implement a shared affectability that facilitates visceral ways of relating to others and that can serve as a prerequisite for building anti-capitalist communal relations across social, identity, and cultural positions (Zink, 2019). Affective communities are attentive to the psychological elements of creating anti-capitalism among groups that may not yet have assumed any kind of organised cohesion (see Bettez & Hytten, 2013). As such, affective communities are able to "join the intimate histories of bodies, with the public domain of justice and injustice" (Ahmed, 2015, p. 202). For those involved in an anti-capitalist psychology of community, affective communities represent under-considered sites that hold the potential to collectivise and politicise formerly disparate bodies (Zink, 2019), binding them—through shared affect—into a politicised multitude (Hardt & Negri, 2004). Although affective communities are temporal in nature, this should not discount their capacity to foster a sustained anti-capitalist political commitment among communities. On the contrary, affective communities can leave an impression of communality that can be retrieved in those moments where capitalism seems most triumphant (Zink, 2019). In other words, affective communities can be drawn on to reactivate people's identification with an anti-capitalist project in moments when such a project seems irretrievable.

It is because issues of justice and oppression are material, psychological, and symbolic that community-building and anti-capitalist politics cannot ignore the role and power that affect has in harnessing the passions which drive political action. With (in)justice and community-building always involving affect (see Ahmed, 2015), affective community-building enables people to interrogate the very communities in which they live out and commit to an anti-capitalist politics (Rowe &

Royster, 2017). Such interrogation is important precisely because it seeks to use different structures of feeling to envision a world beyond the readily available logic of capitalism (Williams, 1977), a logic that informs many of the popular instrumentalist top-down approaches to community-building (e.g. Alinsky, 1971). Psychologists of community are, thus, urged to work with people and the common affect generated in their communities (geographic, social, political, or otherwise) to destabilise fixed or regressive conceptions of belonging in ways that encourage a re-commitment to the actioning of anti-capitalist politics (see Mouffe, 2018). We might, in this sense, conclude that in its rejection of the capitalist forces that disfigure life, affective community-building represents a collective will to life (see Mbembe, 2021).

Issues of Reflexivity

Any anti-capitalist effort to organise politically, affectively build community, or make solidarity does so through intersubjective relations that are not necessarily egalitarian. People do not, in other words, enter into struggle shorn of their social positionalities. They always "bring with them the marks of their origin" (Freire, 1970, p. 36), which can hinder trust, engender suspicions, lead to patronising modes of address, and re-inscribe hierarchical social relations. In addressing the unequal and potentially oppressive patterns of power that exist between comrades, reflexivity denotes the development of a politicised self-awareness that informs the construction of equitable relational networks (see Pillow, 2003). As such, the use of critical reflexivity theory explicates how an individual's subjectivity, life experiences, hermeneutic frame, and approach to politics are linked (Pringle & Thorpe, 2017), thereby assisting in making clear the action that needs to be taken to address the currents of oppressive power that function subtly within anti-capitalist political engagements.

Reflexivity has ushered in a welcome challenge to the positivism and post-positivist approaches that continue to characterise much of mainstream psychology. Our self-location, as psychologists, always affects the work we do, and to deny this can encourage a "universalising practice" that assumes expertise and enacts control over people's lives (see Teo, 2018b). However, even though critically oriented psychologists have a long tradition of using reflexive practice to make visible the ways by which psychological work can inflict harm, such reflexivity seldom results in action which, as Wanda Pillow (2003) reminds us, is a—if not *the*—central tenet of critical reflexivity. When reflexivity is confined to rhetoric that is removed from action, it can legitimise the existence of unequal power relations by simply expressing an awareness of them. Speaking truth to power may, in fact, do very little to change the constitution of power.

As noted in Chap. 2, an anti-capitalist psychology of community occupies an inherently contradictory space (i.e. a commitment to an anti-capitalist politics from within and alongside the discipline of psychology which has, since its inception, served as a tool for capitalism and bolstered itself through capitalist apparatuses). Psychology is, therefore, perhaps unable to fully embody anti-capitalist politics, but a reflexive awareness can help psychologists of community identify and, subsequently, take action to circumvent the neoliberal potentialities of psychology. We can bend psychology in accordance with anti-capitalist politics, rather than psychologise these politics in accordance with psychology's neoliberal mandate. Reflexively interrogating the role that psychology and psychologists play in anti-capitalist activity thus requires that psychologists of community shift psychology's political commitments and alliances in ways that are unlikely to leave us with a discipline that resembles psychology as we have come to understand it (see Clegg & Lansdall-Welfare, 2020).

We are confronted, then, with the question of how those working from within an anti-capitalist psychology of community can advance action-oriented reflexivity that can change not only the discipline of psychology but also how psychology is used and to what effect. Answering this requires that psychologists of community work with anti-capitalist collectives to engage in difficult discussions centring on reflexivity while, at the same time, contributing to these discussions in ways that relinquish the psychologist's role as the Master Knower. Reflexivity requires that psychologists of community working in activist spaces listen and share without dominating these spaces or deferring to the supposed authority of psychology (see Bettez, 2011). This is not to shut down disagreements that psychologists of community have with community activists. On the contrary, psychologists of community should contribute to discussions and offer their skills where necessary (Burton et al., 2012), making clear what their political and subjective positions are, lest these are assumed and/or distorted by those with whom they work (see Cornell et al., 2020). The point, here, is to encourage a self-aware contribution to—rather than a performative disengagement from—anti-capitalist community activity. Psychologists of community can work through the tensions and disagreements of the anti-capitalist collective (contributing and stating their views when appropriate) with self-awareness and contextual sensitivity so that this collective might use these tensions to inform a common set of values and political goals (see Minkler, 2012; Sloan & Brush, 2022). Reflexivity does not call on psychologists of community to reify the activist relation. Instead, it holds those who forge this relation (including psychologists of community) accountable to the anti-capitalist politics they seek to build together. As Achille Mbembe (2021) puts it, reflexive awareness "is not about withdrawing into oneself, about allowing oneself to be inhabited by obsession with one's own place … but rather about contributing to the rise of a new planet where we will all be welcome, where we will all be able to enter unconditionally" (p. 172).

We might think of the sort of reflexive work that occurs within an anti-capitalist psychology of community as *organic reflexivity* (see Malherbe, 2018). What do I mean by this? One embodies the position of an organic intellectual when they assume the role of a permanent persuader who articulates anti-capitalist struggles for the purpose of winning people over to these struggles (see Gramsci, 1971). Those committed to organic reflexivity are, therefore, aware of their potential complicity in the very situation that they seek to change. For the organic intellectual, the politics of anti-capitalist struggle are used to assess the success of reflexivity, rather than relying on moralistic or subjective judgments to do so (see Dean, 2019). It is within organic reflexivity that we can see traces of what Thomas Teo (2018b) calls meta-reflexivity, whereby the emancipatory goals of critical work are, themselves, assessed and held to the critical principles that this work claims to espouse.

While there have been considerable discussions, both within and outside of psychology, on how our conscious actions and subjective privileges can be reflexively interrogated (e.g. in consciousness-raising groups or through "loving critique"; see Chap. 5), I wish to focus here on the importance of the unconscious for advancing organic reflexivity. Indeed, if reflexive work within a psychology of community has attempted to engage in consciousness-raising (e.g. Montero, 1994), there remains much to be done when we consider reflexivity in terms of unconsciousness-raising (see Ryan & Trevithick, 1988). Here, I refer to the Freudian conception of the unconscious as a form of thinking that—despite being internal to the unfolding of conscious or "known" thought—opposes and disturbs such thought (Lear, 2005). Unconsciousness-raising thus entails reflexively interrogating unconscious desire (e.g. by free association or exploring the content of dreams, parapraxes, jokes, and/ or transferences) so that psychologists of community may delve into those unspeakable aspects of themselves that thwart anti-capitalist community work (e.g. their libidinal attachment to the capitalist apparatuses on which their discipline depends, Malherbe, 2021a). To reflexively integrate the unconscious is, effectively, to interrogate what Sandy Lazarus (2018) calls the missionary stance, which denotes how unconscious positions of superiority are adopted by psychologists of community in their well-intentioned attempts to help people. Added to this, when psychologists of community reflexively address their unconscious desires (which may entail working with psychoanalytically trained psychologists of community; see González & Peltz, 2021), they guard against organic reflexivity collapsing into a mere rhetorical recounting of identity markers which rely on notions of a fixable or knowable modernist subject (see Pillow, 2003). A focus on unconscious desire seeks to make conscious the Freudian "return of the repressed" (and how this repressed content is "remembered" in the present through repeated action, Lear, 2005) so that psychologists of community can weaken the regressive influences that the unconscious has on their political activity (see Long, 2021). As Frantz Fanon (1967) argues, we can conscientise the unconscious by reflexively disidentifying with oppressive social structures so that we can more effectively change these structures. In this, psychologists of community can better determine external enemies from the enemy that they make of themselves (see Mbembe, 2019).

As the unconscious is bound up with linguistic practices, it is social in its constitution, meaning that an organically reflexive interrogation of the unconscious can be helpful for activists who are engaged, collectively, in anti-capitalist struggle (Malherbe, 2021a). Psychologists of community (in collaboration with trained psychoanalysts) can work with activists to hold individual desires accountable, rather than repress them, thereby preventing the repeated return of these desires (see Lear, 2005). Organic reflexivity, in this sense, renders the self both collective and social, rejecting discourses of shame, pseudo-radicality, and the mythological "perfect soul" (see Žižek, 1989) for an ongoing reflection that is willed towards making equal—and thus also strengthening and legitimising—the intersubjective bonds upon which the anti-capitalist collective relies. While psychologists of community and the activists with whom they work cannot ever fully *know* their unconscious desires, drawing on psychoanalytic theory to interrogate desire within anti-capitalist reflexive work can facilitate how they take up Pillow's (2003) call to make clear that the unfamiliar is precisely that: unfamiliar. As such, psychologists and activists can move towards altering the power that unconscious thinking has on political action and in this reject the limits of "reflexive knowing" (see Pringle & Thorpe, 2017) as well as a circular—potentially pleasurable—kind of self-conscious reflection that serves to protect individual guilt (Lear, 2005).

Although reflexivity is not a substitute for anti-capitalist action, organic reflexivity can inform how people commit to and enact this action so that it reflects a democratic, empathetic, egalitarian, and socially just ethos. Changing the oppressive social structures of the neoliberal political project requires that we work with one another to build a common anti-capitalist project. Doing so means that we must reflexively address how the oppressive structures of capitalism (including racism and sexism) take hold of our being at both conscious and unconscious levels. This is challenging work. As Niklas Luhmann (1985) writes, the paradox of reflection is that it desires unity but produces difference. It is, therefore, through organically reflexive processes that an anti-capitalist psychology of community can assist activists and psychologists of community to take up this challenge and implement what Pillow (2003) calls "reflexivities of discomfort" (p. 187), whereby currents of oppressive power within anti-capitalist movements are grappled with in a manner that encourages action and solidarity.

Case Illustration: Connection and Antagonism

In an attempt to make clear the connections between the different anti-capitalist approaches outlined in this chapter, and to flesh out some of the more theoretical components of these approaches, I look in this section to my own community-engaged work. This work, which I believe is exemplary of an anti-capitalist psychology of community, comes out of a 35-year partnership between the University of South Africa's Institute for Social and Health Sciences (ISHS) and residents from Thembelihle, a low-income community located in south-west Johannesburg. Although I will speak more about Thembelihle in Chap. 4 and Chap. 5, for now, I will simply note that since its establishment in 1989, Thembelihle has presented a very particular history of anti-capitalist struggle, usually through protests and campaigns directed against neoliberal austerity policies (Ngwane, 2021). Today, the community is considered one of Johannesburg's 22 "protest hotspots" (Tselapedi & Dugard, 2013). Resultantly, activists from Thembelihle have, over the years, faced immense brutality from the South African Police Service and even the South African Army (Poplak, 2015). Yet, despite the particularities of its struggle history,

Thembelihle is indicative of how neoliberal policy has, since 1996, disproportionately affected South Africa's Black working class and poor population (Duncan,
2016; Suffla et al., 2020). Like so many other poor communities in the country, even
the most basic of public services (e.g. sanitation, paved roads, electrification) remain
partial—if not altogether absent—in Thembelihle (Suffla et al., 2020).

In 2016, around 24 residents from Thembelihle partnered with a film production
company, myself, and several others from the ISHS to produce a documentary film
that sought to tell stories of Thembelihle from the perspectives of those who live and
work there. As detailed elsewhere (see Malherbe, Seedat, et al., 2021b), where some
community members were involved in producing and editing the film, determining
its overall focus and representational accent, others appeared in the film itself. The
final film product, which community members titled *Thembelihle: Place of Hope*, is
just over 25 minutes long and depicts quotidian and political life in the community,
as well as its histories of struggle. It does so through the voices of a small-scale
farmer, a peer educator, a scrapyard owner, a dancer, two activists, a shop owner, a
brick-maker, two nurses, a football coach, and a kindergarten principal. In an
attempt to organise politically around the different—often disparate—struggles represented in the documentary, community members partnered with ISHS staff to host
several public screenings in and beyond Thembelihle.

Community-engaged projects, such as this one, are not inherently anti-capitalist,
nor are they necessarily psychological in their orientation. Therefore, the task of an
anti-capitalist psychology of community is to draw out a project's psychosocial
valances and connect these with existing and nascent anti-capitalist action. In this
participatory film project, several activist groups—such as the Thembelihle Crisis
Committee (or TCC, a "socialist-oriented" political movement organisation that has
been operating since 2001 and has organised protests for housing, sanitation, electricity, and other social services, Ngwane, 2021, p. 144) as well as the Thembelihle
Women's Forum (a small group of women concerned with advancing gender equity
in Thembelihle, Day, 2021)—were invited to attend different public screenings and
to discuss their political agendas in relation to the documentary. The screenings
thereby served as platforms for communicating and connecting different anti-
capitalist struggles in the community. Members of the Women's Forum, for instance,
related their struggles for social reproduction rights to the narratives of the kindergarten principal and the nurses in the documentary. TCC activists similarly linked
their campaigns for safe public infrastructure, housing, and reliable public services
to the plight of the farmer, the activists, and the bricklayers. At one screening, when
a younger audience member asked "What can we do because we've seen the documentary? We've seen the challenges, but how do we fix it? We still have [to develop]
a programme and we still have a lot to do in Thembelihle", an activist from TCC
responded to this question by outlining TCC's anti-capitalist programme. Audiences
were thus made aware of the kinds of organised anti-capitalist activity with which
they could become involved, and, as such, different social movements were able to
strengthen themselves by drawing on the visceral and emotional qualities of the
documentary (i.e. its engagement with different structures of feeling in Thembelihle).

It was in these ways that those working on the participatory film project could use the screening events to harness institutional resources (e.g. transportation, communications, food, a venue) for anti-capitalist organising.

The public screenings also served to build the solidarity relation in particular ways. For example, in addition to audience members expressing interest in becoming involved in TCC's anti-capitalist organising, several audience members noted that they had changed their view of TCC, which has been consistently represented in mainstream South African media as an organisation defined by little other than meaningless violence (see Malherbe, Seedat, et al., 2021b). It became clear that TCC's anti-capitalist agenda was concerned primarily with dignity and a better life for all: a project to which many audience members were prepared to offer their solidarity.

Outside of the formal project parameters, activists from TCC screened the documentary to other anti-capitalist movements from surrounding communities, wherein the purpose was, as one TCC activist explained to me, to articulate Thembelihle's contemporary and historical anti-capitalist struggles in an emotionally appealing way and thus create avenues for solidarity-making through what I am calling affective communities. In an example of militant particularism, the infra-community connections facilitated at these screening events saw different activist groups link their struggles with those of others, thereby developing a broad-based "culture of solidarity" (Ngwane, 2021, p. 10). Solidarity was, in this respect, not built on the presumption of identical suffering, but on a chain of equivalence where different experiences of alienation were connected to form a coalition against a common experience of alienation under capitalism.

The solidarity relation was also built at smaller screenings (e.g. among cultural workers and feminist groups), where post-screening discussions were concerned with the conditions on which audience members would build solidarity with anti-capitalist groups like TCC. For some, solidarity would only be offered when the leaders of groups like TCC demonstrated greater respect for rank-and-file cadres, while for others it was necessary that these groups take the emancipation of women, migrants, and children more seriously. It was thus at these smaller screenings that the fetishisation of the solidarity relation was rejected in a manner that nonetheless stressed the importance of this relation for anti-capitalist organising.

With representation being a crucial determinant in the spreading of affect (Wetherell, 2015), many of the screening events served as spaces for affective community-building. A number of audience members expressed feeling connected to those around them through the pride that they felt in seeing the victories that anti-capitalist struggle in Thembelihle had won (e.g. partial electrification in 2016; see Ngwane, 2021) and how community activists had worked together to address internal problems (e.g. spates of xenophobic violence; see Malherbe, Seedat, et al., 2021b). Such affective connections were important for generating meaningful solidarity relationships among organised anti-capitalist movements in the community, as well as winning the solidarity and support of those outside of these movements. These affective communities, temporary as they may have been, were then reactivated over a series of screening events (there were groups of people who attended almost every screening), meaning that long-term organisational activities took place within and through a particular affective community. However, not all the affective communities that were constructed at the screenings were of a positive nature (which is not to say that they were not meaningful in some way). For instance, it was clear that the anti-capitalist activism with which community members were involved (some for over three decades) had taken a psychological toll. As one audience member noted with regard to the material struggles that were depicted in the documentary, "I saw that you [community members involved in producing the documentary] have shown us the water and the mud. These are things that are affecting people psychologically". Audience members were able to feel in common as well as alongside one another in their experiences of capitalism and anti-capitalist activism. There was, resultantly, much discussion on how mental health services remain a neglected political demand by anti-capitalist movements in Thembelihle.

The screening events were not without moments of tension and disagreement. At one event, there was an especially heated debate between young activists who rejected the role of the South African State within anti-capitalist struggle and older activists who maintained that the State is useful for actioning grassroots anti-capitalist demands. In other instances, there were debates on how Thembelihle was represented in the documentary and what use these representations could be for anti-capitalist movements. Some vehemently rejected what they described as "the face of poverty" portrayed in the documentary, while others celebrated how the "reality of poverty" was coupled with the documentary's humanistic depiction of community, as noted by one audience member who proclaimed, "it felt good for me - or us - as Thembelihle, just to see and show other people inside of Thembelihle that it's not all that bad, and that there is good". Although the debates at the screening events were often uncomfortable and psychologically demanding (one audience member spoke about being "emotionally triggered" by some of the debates), and they were rarely resolved, they were useful for addressing some of the contradictions inherent to anti-capitalist organising. It soon became clear that anti-capitalist collaboration depended not on doing away with these contradictions through a falsely unifying synthesis, but on the strategic deployment of these contradictory strategies. For example, although TCC activists rejected the State when it came to issues of food security during the COVID-19 pandemic (working instead with the ISHS and non-governmental organisations, like the Gift of the Givers Foundation, to initiate mutual aid food drives), they held the State accountable for payment packages during the country's lockdown period. It was, therefore, possible to engage critically with different tactics and work with those with whom one disagrees politically to advance anti-capitalist programmes.

The kinds of organically reflexive engagement apparent at many of the screenings were, for me, especially demonstrative of how a psychology of community could be used to strengthen the intersubjective relations that constitute anti-capitalist initiatives. For example, the representations of social reproduction (especially the care work undertaken by the nurses and teachers in the documentary; see Chap. 5) brought feminised labour into the consciousness of several male anti-capitalists who were moved to discuss how this had been neglected in their political thinking and activism. My status as a White, educated, and middle-class outsider was also brought into several screening discussions. One audience member, for example, proclaimed that White people had, for so long, played a central role in disenfranchising Thembelihle and that the screening spaces felt inauthentic when they were facilitated by a White person (i.e. me) who was so removed from the community's history as well as its present-day linguistic, cultural, and material realities. This raised important questions around the ownership of the project. As such, I ensured that my presence at documentary screenings would be one that was invited rather than assumed (I was, for instance, not invited to the screenings that the TCC hosted with other anti-capitalist groups). Moreover, observations such as these led me to probe into the unconscious desires that I, as a community psychologist, may have had when working on a project such as this. Certainly, I benefited considerably from this project (e.g. I have received numerous publications and a university degree from it). It would, therefore, be disingenuous to ignore how my involvement in this project has bolstered my own cultural capital. It was important, though, that such reflexivity did not debilitate my engagement with the community. Instead, it was to serve as a point of reflection that informed my commitment to the anti-capitalist struggles being expressed at the screenings. If I was to be useful to these struggles in some way, I certainly could not engage with the community as an insider, but I also could not do so as an outsider too debilitated by guilt and/or feelings of inauthenticity to act. My engagement thus depended on my status as a particular subject with access to particular knowledges and resources. I was, therefore, guided by various anti-capitalist collectives and other community members as to how these knowledges and resources could be used to advance their struggles (e.g. which resources should be made available at screenings; strategic places at which to host screenings; which politicians and journalists should be invited to screenings and which should not; and how I could assist in facilitating post-screening political meetings). The point, then, was not to construct the perfect comrade subjectivity, but to work out what was required from me as a particular politically committed subject.

People feel and experience capitalism on physical and psychological levels. These feelings cannot be ignored by anti-capitalist movements that seek to garner broad-based appeal. At one of the last in-person screenings that occurred before the COVID-19 pandemic, an audience member commented that "There are many … who are at this present moment, even if you are talking with [us] about life and football, they take you and discuss [economic] underdevelopment because this thing is affecting them, mentally, spiritually. It is psychological". Indeed, the documentary screenings were able to evoke the psycho-material character of anti-capitalism, articulating its affective and emotional forms for purposes of political organising and solidarity-building. This process was characterised by tensions, intense affect, and reflexive introspection, all of which guided how an anti-capitalist psychology of community was employed.

Conclusion

To resist the neoliberal political project is to reject teleology and intervene in the stifling futures that are made available by this project. Undoubtedly, our "future does not automatically unfold from the present" (Ratner, 2019, p. 180). In this chapter, I have attempted to demonstrate how a psychology of community can be used to advance anti-capitalist struggle through political organising, solidarity-making, affective community-building, and critical reflexivity. Although I have focused on anti-capitalist social movements, there are certainly many other areas in which an anti-capitalist psychology of community can be used for purposes of resisting the neoliberal project, including struggles in the workplace, in the market, and in the domestic sphere (see Harvey, 2020). In short, I have only begun to penetrate the surface of how an anti-capitalist psychology of community can be used "dangerously" to establish new, more equitable social relations which are made structurally impossible by a capitalist political economy (see Roberts, 2015).

References

Ahmed, S. (2015). *The cultural politics of emotion*. Routledge.
Alinsky, S. (1971). *Rules for radicals*. Random House.
Amin, S. (2014). *The implosion of capitalism*. Pluto Press.
Bettez, S. C. (2011). Critical community building: Beyond belonging. *Educational Foundations, 25*, 3–19.
Bettez, S. C., & Hytten, K. (2013). Community building in social justice work: A critical approach. *Educational Studies, 49*(1), 45–66.
Brodsky, A. E., & Faryal, T. (2006). No matter how hard you try, your feet still get wet: Insider and outsider perspectives on bridging diversity. *American Journal of Community Psychology, 37*(3–4), 191–201.
Burton, M., Kagan, C., & Duckett, P. (2012). Making the psychological political–challenges for community psychology. *Global Journal of Community Psychology Practice, 3*, 1–11.
Carriere, K. R. (2020). Workers' rights are human rights: Organizing the psychology of labor movements. *Current Opinion in Psychology, 35*, 60–64.
Clegg, J. A., & Lansdall-Welfare, R. (2020). Psychology and neoliberalism. In W. Pickren (Ed.), *Encyclopedia of the history of psychology*. Oxford University Press.
Cornell, J., Seedat, M., Malherbe, N., & Suffla, S. (2020). Splintered politics of memory and community resistance. *Journal of Community Psychology, 48*(5), 1677–1695.
Cox, L. (2011). *How do we keep going? Activist burnout and sustainability in social movements*. Into-ebooks.
Davis, A. Y. (2016). *Freedom is a constant struggle: Ferguson, Palestine, and the foundations of a movement*. Haymarket Books.
Day, S. (2021). *Women's everyday resistance: Space, affect and healing* (Doctoral dissertation, University of South Africa, Pretoria, South Africa). Retrieved from uir.unisa.ac.za/bitstream/handle/10500/27717/thesis_day_s.pdf?sequence=1
Dean, J. (2019). *Comrade: An essay on political belonging*. Verso.
Debord, G. (1977). *Society of the spectacle*. Black & Red.
Duncan, J. (2016). *Protest nation: The right to protest in South Africa*. University of KwaZulu-Natal Press.

Fanon, F. (1967). *Black skin, white masks*. Grove Press.

Featherstone, D. (2012). *Solidarity: Hidden histories and geographies of internationalism*. Zed Books.

Fourie, E., & Terre Blanche, M. (2019). About accountants and translators: Reshaping community engagement in South African psychology. *South Africa Journal of Psychology, 49*(1), 39–51.

Fox, D. (2011). Anarchism and psychology. *Theory in Action, 4*(4), 31–48.

Fraser, N. (2014). Behind Marx's hidden abode. *New Left Review, 85*(2), 55–74.

Freeman, J. (1972). The tyranny of structurelessness. In A. Koedt, E. Levine, & A. Rapone (Eds.), *Radical feminism* (pp. 285–299). Quadrangle.

Freire, P. (1970). *Pedagogy of the oppressed*. Herder & Herder.

Fromm, E. (1942). *Fear of freedom*. Routledge.

Gramsci, A. (1971). *Selections from the prison notebooks*. Lawrence & Wishart.

González, F. J., & Peltz, R. (2021). Community psychoanalysis: Collaborative practice as intervention. *Psychoanalytic Dialogues, 31*(4), 409–427.

Han, B. (2017). *Psychopolitics: Neoliberalism and new technologies of power*. Verso.

Hannah, S. (2021). *Why we need anti-capitalist resistance*. Resistance Books.

Hardt, M., & Negri, A. (2004). *Multitude*. Penguin Books.

Hardt, M., & Negri, A. (2009). *Commonwealth*. Harvard University Press.

Hardt, M., & Negri, A. (2017). *Assembly*. Oxford University Press.

Harrell, S. P., & Bond, M. A. (2006). Listening to diversity stories: Principles for practice in community research and action. *American Journal of Community Psychology, 37*(3–4), 365–376.

Harris, A. (2018). Emotions, feelings, and social change: Love, anger, and solidarity in black women's AIDS activism. *Women, Gender, and Families of Color, 6*(2), 181–201.

Harvey, D. (2017). *The ways of the world*. Profile Books.

Harvey, D. (2020). *The anti-capitalist chronicles*. Pluto Press.

Laclau, E., & Mouffe, C. (1985). *Hegemony and socialist strategy: Towards a radical democratic politics*. Verso.

Latham, R. (2018). Contemporary capitalism, uneven development, and the arc of anti-capitalism. *Global Discourse, 8*(2), 169–186.

Latif, N., & Latif, L. (2016, November 22). 'We know what it is to bury a child'–The black mothers turning mourning into a movement. *The Guardian*. Retrieved from https://www.theguardian.com/world/2016/nov/22/mothers-of-the-movement-trayvon-martin-sandra-bland-eric-garner-amadou-diallo-sean-bell

Lazarus, S. (2018). *Power and identity in the struggle for social justice: Reflections on community psychology practice*. Springer.

Lazarus, S., Seedat, M., & Naidoo, T. (2017). Community building: Challenges of constructing community. In M. Bond, I. Serrano-Garcia, C. B. Keys, & M. Shinn (Eds.), *APA handbook of community psychology: Vol. 2. Methods for community research and action for diverse groups and issues (pp. 215–234)*. American Psychological Association.

Luhmann, N. (1985). Die autopoiesis des bewusstseins. *Soziale Welt, 36*, 402–446.

Lear, J. (2005). *Freud*. Routledge.

Long, W. (2021). *Nation on the couch: Inside South Africa's mind*. Melinda Ferguson Books.

Malherbe, N. (2018). Expanding conceptions of liberation: Holding Marxisms with liberation psychology. *Theory & Psychology, 28*(3), 340–357.

Malherbe, N. (2020). Articulating liberation psychologies of culture. *Journal of Theoretical and Philosophical Psychology, 40*(4), 203–218.

Malherbe, N. (2021a). A psychopolitical interpretation of de-alienation: Marxism, psychoanalysis, and liberation psychology. *Psychoanalysis, Culture & Society, 26*(3), 263–283.

Malherbe, N. (2021b). Considering love: Implications for critical political psychology. *New Ideas in Psychology, 61*, 100851.

Malherbe, N., & Dlamini, S. (2020). Troubling history and diversity: Disciplinary decadence in community psychology. *Community Psychology in Global Perspective, 6*(2/1), 144–157.

Malherbe, N., Ratele, K., Adams, G., Reddy, G., & Suffla, S. (2021a). A decolonial Africa(n)-centered psychology of antiracism. *Review of General Psychology, 25*(4), 437–450.

Malherbe, N., Seedat, M., & Suffla, S. (2021b). Understanding community violence: A critical realist framework for community psychology. *Journal of Community Psychology*. Advance online publication https://doi.org/10.1002/jcop.22660.

Mannarini, T., & Salvatore, S. (2019). Making sense of ourselves and others: A contribution to the community-diversity debate. *Community Psychology in Global Perspective, 5*(1), 26–37.

Mbembe, A. (2019). *Necropolitics*. Wits University Press.

Mbembe, A. (2021). *Out of the dark night: Essays on decolonization*. Wits University Press.

Minkler, M. (2012). Introduction to community organizing and community-building. In M. Minkler (Ed.), *Community organizing and community-building for health and welfare* (pp. 5–26). Rutgers University Press.

Montero, M. (1994). Consciousness raising, conversion, and de-ideologization in community psychosocial work. *Journal of Community Psychology, 22*(1), 3–11.

Mouffe, C. (2018). *For a left populism*. Verso.

Ndelu, S., Dlakavu, S., & Boswell, B. (2017). Womxn's and nonbinary activists' contribution to the RhodesMustFall and FeesMustFall student movements: 2015 and 2016. *Agenda, 31*(3–4), 1–4.

Ndlovu-Gatsheni, S. J. (2021). Revisiting Marxism and decolonisation through the legacy of Samir Amin. *Review of African Political Economy, 48*(167), 50–65.

Negri, A. (2008). *Goodbye Mr socialism: Radical politics in the 21st century*. Serpent's Tail.

Nelson, G., & Prilleltensky, I. (2010). *Community psychology: In pursuit of liberation and wellbeing (2nd Ed)*. Palgrave Macmillan.

Ngwane, T. (2021). *Amakomiti: Grassroots democracy in South African shack settlements*. Pluto Press.

Oyakawa, M., McKenna, E., & Han, H. (2021). Habits of courage: Reconceptualizing risk in social movement organizing. *Journal of Community Psychology, 49*(8), 3101–3121.

Pillow, W. (2003). Confession, catharsis, or cure? Rethinking the uses of reflexivity as methodological power in qualitative research. *International Journal of Qualitative Studies in Education, 16*(2), 175–196.

Poplak, R. (2015, May 5). The army vs. Thembelihle: Where the truth lies. *Daily Maverick*. Retrieved from https://www.dailymaverick.co.za/article/2015-05-05-the-army-vsthembelihle-where-the-truth-lies/

Pringle, R., & Thorpe, H. (2017). Theory and reflexivity. In M. L. Silk, D. L. Andrews, & H. Thorpe (Eds.), *Routledge handbook of physical cultural studies* (pp. 32–41). Routledge.

Ratner, C. (2019). *Neoliberal psychology*. Springer.

Roberts, R. (2015). *Psychology and capitalism: The manipulation of mind*. Zero Books.

Rowe, A. C., & Royster, F. T. (2017). Loving transgressions: Queer of color bodies, affective ties, transformative community. *Journal of Lesbian Studies, 21*(3), 243–253.

Ryan, J., & Trevithick, P. A. (1988). Unconsciousness raising with working class women. In S. Krzowski & P. Land (Eds.), *Our experience: Workshops at the women's therapy Centre* (pp. 63–83). Women's Press.

Sloan, T., & Brush, J. (2022). Supporting activists and progressive social movements. In C. Walker, S. Zlotowitz, & A. Zoli (Eds.), *The Palgrave handbook of innovative community and clinical psychologies* (pp. 101–120). Palgrave Macmillan.

Suffla, S., Malherbe, N., & Seedat, M. (2020). Recovering the everyday within and for decolonial peacebuilding through politico-affective space. In Y. G. Acar, S. M. Moss, & O. M. Uluğ (Eds.), *Researching peace, conflict, and power in the field: Methodological challenges and opportunities* (pp. 343–364). Springer.

Teo, T. (2018a). Homo neoliberalus: From personality to forms of subjectivity. *Theory & Psychology, 28*(5), 581–599.

Teo, T. (2018b). *Outline of theoretical psychology: Critical investigations*. Palgrave Macmillan.

Tselapedi, T., & Dugard, J. (2013). Reclaiming power: A case study of the Thembelihle crisis committee. *Good Governance Learning Network*. Retrieved from https://ggln.org.za/images/solg_reports/SoLG_2013.pdf#page=58

Von Scheve, V. (2019). Social collectives. In J. Slaby & C. von Scheve (Eds.), *Affective societies: Key concepts* (pp. 267–278). Routledge.

Walter, C. L., & Hyde, C. A. (2012). Community building practice: An expanded conceptual framework. In M. Minkler (Ed.), *Community organizing and community building for health and welfare* (pp. 78–93). Rutgers University Press.

Wetherell, M. (2015). Trends in the turn to affect: A social psychological critique. *Body & Society, 21*(2), 139–166.

Wilkinson, E. (2017). On love as an (im)properly political concept. *Environment and Planning D: Society and Space, 35*(1), 57–71.

Williams, R. (1977). *Marxism and literature*. Oxford University Press.

Williams, R. (2016). *Resources of hope: Culture, democracy, socialism*. Verso.

Wright, E. O. (2015). *Understanding class*. Verso.

Wright, E. O. (2019). *How to be an anti-capitalist in the 21st century*. Verso.

Yeros, P., & Jha, P. (2020). Late neo-colonialism: Monopoly capitalism in permanent crisis. *Agrarian South: Journal of Political Economy, 9*(1), 78–93.

Zink, V. (2019). Affective communities. In J. Slaby & C. Von Scheve (Eds.), *Affective societies: Key concepts* (pp. 289–299). Routledge.

Žižek, S. (1989). *The sublime object of ideology*. Verso.

Žižek, S. (2020). *A left that dares to speak its name: 34 untimely interventions*. Polity.

Chapter 4
Resisting Capitalist Ideology

As outlined in Chap. 2, neoliberal ideology can be understood as a social process that eliminates the structural contradictions of capitalism and the individual subject by presenting these contradictions as external differences that should be either tolerated or overcome with hard work (see McGowan, 2019). As such, neoliberal ideology presents itself as reality—how things *really are*—rather than an ideology (Ratner, 2019) and impels people to accept capitalism as it is, condemning any vision of an alternative future as, itself, ideological (Žižek, 2020). Neoliberal ideology, in essence, ensures that being and seeing align with an ethic of accumulation and profit-making (see Ailon, 2022).

In this chapter, I explore how psychologists of community can contribute to an anti-capitalist conception of what Ignacio Martín-Baró (1994) called de-ideologisation, that is, a process of retrieving people's experiences beyond the ideological reference points of the elite classes. I argue that de-ideologisation, when placed within an anti-capitalist frame, re-symbolises neoliberal ideology, making clear its constitutive contradictions so that we might act upon them (Malherbe, 2021b). I then expound upon three modes of re-symbolisation that can be taken up by those involved in an anti-capitalist psychology of community, namely, transforming subjectivities, creating art in accordance with the popular aesthetic, and retrieving cultural memory. None of these re-symbolising efforts are, in themselves, sufficient for the development of an anti-capitalist politics. Yet, as Edward Said (1993) reminds us, "primary" resistance against an oppressive political economy (see Chap. 3) always requires a complementary ideological resistance that restores severed community relations and revitalises politically dissident energies. Anti-capitalism is, then, undoubtedly a political problem, but it is also a problem of thinking, relating, imagining, and symbolising (see Watkins & Shulman, 2008), meaning that it is a problem of ideology. As such, ideological critique is essential for building a political culture—within and across communities—that informs and renders appealing organised anti-capitalist movements.

What Does It Mean to Re-symbolise Neoliberal Ideology?

Anti-capitalist de-ideologisation is concerned with re-symbolisation, which seeks to reinterpret the world and the subjects who act in and on this world in terms of contradiction (Malherbe, 2021b), thereby combatting neoliberal ideology's attempt

N. Malherbe, *For an Anti-capitalist Psychology of Community*, Community Psychology, https://doi.org/10.1007/978-3-030-99696-3_4

at "resolving" contradiction through the free market. In other words, because neither the self nor society is at one with themselves (see Chaps. 1 and 2), re-symbolisation requires that we demonstrate how capitalism moves through contradiction. It is, then, through re-symbolisation that contradiction can be used to drive anti-capitalist action by rejecting the false promises and static subjectivities offered by neoliberal ideology. As we shall see, the purpose of anti-capitalist re-symbolisation is not to overwhelm people with an awareness of contradiction, nor is it to point towards a life beyond contradiction (Malherbe, 2021b). Instead, using contradiction for anti-capitalist re-symbolisation attunes people to not only who is being oppressed (Said, 1993) but how ideology works, materially, to sustain the social divisions which drive this oppression (see Ghosh, 2021; Marx & Engels, 1968).

By centralising contradiction in anti-capitalist communicative strategies, re-symbolisation is alive to confrontation and antagonism and thus seeks to name the enemies of anti-capitalism (Žižek, 2020). Psychologists of community can work with activists to foster political education in ways that do not make contradiction a point of shame or take it as a sign of incompleteness, but as an indication of the gaps and weaknesses inherent to neoliberal ideology, thereby revealing how this ideology fails by its own logic and, therefore, how it can be attacked effectively (McGowan, 2019; Pavón-Cuéllar, 2017). For instance, neoliberal ideology's meritocratic quilting point is rendered illegitimate when political educators focus on how the backbreaking labour of the majority serves as the condition for the wealth of a small minority (i.e. material reality reveals the contradictions of neoliberal ideology), meaning that such wealth belongs to the producers from whom it is taken. Yet, as Srnicek and Williams (2015) argue, "A politics that finds its best expression in the breakdown of social and economic order is not an alternative" (p. 39). Accordingly, re-symbolisation does not identify and exacerbate contradiction for its own sake, but looks to embolden anti-capitalist action via an awareness of the urgency of such action.

Re-symbolisation, as I have described it above, seeks to establish a new actional language (i.e. a mode of expression that is tied in with doing) that is based on contradiction and that does not attempt the impossible task of distilling the full meaning of political subjects or society through fixed symbols (see Malherbe, 2021b). Rather, this actional language endeavours to lay bare the instability of neoliberal ideology and make perceptible a more equitable existence that lies beyond neoliberalism's ideological strictures (see Ghosh, 2021). In this regard, the repressive tolerance and permissiveness that defines neoliberal ideology are rejected, and truth is located in an anti-capitalist political cause that is sensitive to and moves through contradiction (both external and internal to this cause), thereby redefining notions of the good life in ways that reach beyond people's individualised and immediate interests (see McGowan, 2019). In light of this, an anti-capitalist psychology of community is less concerned with the talking cure than it is with working with people to forge new ways of talking, based on contradiction, that can inform anti-capitalist action (action which is, itself, conceived of as a socially just intervention into contradiction, rather than a neatly synthesising solution to contradiction).

Psychologists of community involved in re-symbolising efforts can work with people to make clear how material exploitation affects subjective perception, using contradiction as a lens through which to understand and make connections between the two. Engaging with contradictions within psychologically oriented spaces requires that people confront the fact that although no society, political project, or social movement can deliver psychic wholeness, we should not tolerate a society whose ethical determinants lie within a dehumanising, alienating neoliberal ideology (see Ailon, 2022). Our psychic alienation can occur within more equitable and dignified social arrangements (Malherbe, 2021b), and it is in this respect that psychologists of community can work with people to interrogate their subjective contradictions in ways that do away with the idea that contradictions represent failures that must be resolved (an idea that remains rampant in much psychological discourse; see Parker, 2011; Pavón-Cuéllar, 2017) and instead draws on the contradictions which mark both subject and society as instances of self-reflection that can inform how one participates in anti-capitalist struggle.

Re-symbolisation uses contradiction to embolden an anti-capitalist political agenda by revealing the contradictions of neoliberal ideology and as such speaks to people's material realities, names ideological enemies, unsettles subjectivities, and expands the horizons of political possibility. In short, re-symbolisation is an attempt to speak differently so that we can think in a manner more aligned with material reality than our ideological opponents who are committed to managing and synthesising contradiction through the so-called free market. In the following three sections, I attempt to demonstrate how an anti-capitalist psychology of community can use re-symbolising strategies to transform subjectivities, recover cultural memory, and create artwork attuned to the popular aesthetic.

Transforming Subjectivities

Under neoliberal ideology, subjective reproduction reflects the alienating conditions of material and social reproduction (Parker, 2011). Marx recognised this when he wrote that the capitalist mode of production "not only creates an object for the subject, but also a subject for the object" (Marx, 1973, p. 92). An anti-capitalist psychology of community must, therefore, begin by recognising the change-making potential that "lies in the possibility of problematising and challenging hegemonic forms of subjectivity" (Kessi & Boonzaier, 2018, p. 303). Even more than this though, because a new politics requires new demands and, therefore, new subjects (Eagleton, 1976), psychologists of community can contribute to the task of remaking subjectivity by working with people to de-link their being from having and to conceive of the self as a process that is always reformed and dispersed through others, objects, psychic states, political commitments, and actions (González Rey, 2016; Rutherford, 2018; Teo, 2018). Although subjectivity cannot be entirely prefigured (Parker, 2011), psychologists of community can work with activists to seize from neoliberal ideology control over the production of subjectivities (see Hardt & Negri, 2009).

Understanding how the outside gets inside of us (i.e. the neoliberalisation of subjectivity) does not, of course, change the outside (Rutherford, 2018; Teo, 2018). We can only transform neoliberal subjectivity by transforming the larger neoliberal political project (see Chap. 3). Yet, at the same time, changing neoliberal society is always connected to the changing of neoliberal subjectivity. The world changes in reaction to subjects and, like subjects, the world is not immovable or fixed (Tanggaard, 2013). Materiality is bound up with how human subjectivities are lived out (Hook, 2013). By engaging subjectivity in relation to democratically constructed anti-capitalist values, we can begin to re-symbolise being in ways that assist us in seeing, moving, and building beyond the narrow realities made possible by neoliberal ideology: a reality where failing economically (as the majority inevitably do) is to fail subjectively. When "we think from our misfitting" (Holloway, 2010, p. 9), we reject the subjectivities that neoliberal ideology and mainstream psychology require and assume (see Pavón-Cuéllar, 2017). In turn, we can shift the source of our subjective hail away from neoliberal ideology and towards the values of an anti-capitalist political project whose ethical coordinates reject those of the neoliberal free market (Ailon, 2022; Malherbe, 2021a).

An anti-capitalist psychology of community can open up spaces for activists to re-symbolise the subjective and ethical consequences of their politics (e.g. how might disciplined political commitment influence who we are and what we desire?) and to refine these politics in ways that reject neoliberal ideologies and our enjoyment of neoliberal subjectivities (e.g. working for political movements should not hail and psychically reward subjects in the same ways that neoliberal ideology does). Reflecting on how political activity produces subjectivities can enable activists to produce subjectivities that are always-becoming, rather than static or fixed, and that are realised, with others, in the process of building of anti-capitalism (Hardt & Negri, 2009). Such work is not always easy because it demands that people break from the secure identifications offered by neoliberal ideology's subjective hail (Fromm, 1942). Yet, when the contradictions and failures of neoliberal subjectivity are worked through and re-symbolised, activists can produce modes of identification that neoliberal ideology simply cannot (e.g. kinship, connectedness, mutual aid). In other words, who we are—our subjectivity—can be transformed through a consciousness of belonging (see Balibar, 1995). When this consciousness is developed in relation to an anti-capitalist politics, new subjective hails are created which, together, reveal the shared sense of humanity that has been structurally disfigured by neoliberal ideology.

So far, I have argued that comrades always make and remake one another as subjects when they are collectively committed to an anti-capitalist project (Dean, 2019). An anti-capitalist psychology of community can thus be used to create spaces for activists to reflect on and intervene in the way that subjectivities are produced within political struggle. One's awareness of and engagement with the subjective configurations that emerge in struggle can lead to new, action-oriented desires for real-world change (González Rey, 2016), or, as Marx and Engels wrote (1968): "in revolutionary activity the changing of oneself coincides with the changing of [one's] circumstances" (p. 29). History has shown us many examples of this. David

Featherstone (2012) demonstrates how, in twentieth-century Britain, the decolonising struggles waged by Black comrades from the Caribbean created solidaritous, anti-racist subjectivities among White maritime trade unionists. In their study with anti-capitalist activists, Katarzyna Jasko et al. (2019) found that the sense of significance that people felt when engaging in political action resulted in an increased likelihood for self-sacrifice to a political cause. Individual subjectivities, when made in struggle contexts, were thus hailed as belonging to and working for the social advancement of the anti-capitalist collective. Forging subjectivity through solidarity-in-struggle in these ways can move subjects to assert that they do not recognise themselves in neoliberal interpellation. The fixed subjectivities hailed by neoliberal ideology are, in this sense, transformed into revolutionary becomings that seek autonomy from capitalist powers and that strive towards another existence that embodies Frantz Fanon's (1967) new humanism (see also Hardt & Negri, 2009). As Wahbie Long (2021) asserts, it is due to their expertise in empathetic listening, communicating, and relating that psychologists are well-placed to assist anti-capitalist collectives in such a radically imaginative humanist project. Although a psychology of community cannot create revolutionary subjectivities, it can facilitate the kinds of collective reflection required for making revolutions in subjectivity (Parker, 2011). An anti-capitalist psychology of community is tasked with ensuring that those moments, within struggle, where revolutionary subjectivities are hailed—even momentarily—are not lost and that activists work together to ensure that their anti-capitalist activities are structured to facilitate the creation of such subjectivities.

It should be noted that creating revolutions in subjectivity is not to engage in the impossible task of settling the fractured self. Pathologising contradictions within subjectivity has long been the ambition of a mainstream psychology concerned with fixing the subject so that there is no need to transform the world (Pavón-Cuéllar, 2017). An anti-capitalist psychology of community must avoid this regressive disciplinary impulse at all costs. We need not realise fantasies of a coherent revolutionary subjectivity nor fetishise victimisation in ways that determine subjectivity and desire through persecution alone (Long, 2021; Mbembe & Rendall, 2002). Rather, an anti-capitalist psychology of community can be drawn on to set in motion and re-symbolise new forms of self-styling that embrace contradiction and that are derived from (and can, in turn, inform) anti-capitalist politics (see Mbembe & Rendall, 2002). Put differently, psychologists of community can work with activists to create coalitions between diverse subjectivities which are, themselves, formed through anti-capitalist political action and organising. It is with such action that we can echo the revolutionary subjectivities of the Zapatistas in Mexico, whose anti-capitalism is premised not on being who they are, but on becoming what they want (Hardt & Negri, 2009).

We do not always know exactly how neoliberal ideology affects the formation of subjective selves. This means that the unconscious cannot go unattended when seeking to transform neoliberal subjectivities (see also Chap. 3). We must break not only with the material ways by which neoliberal subjectivities are constituted but also with the unconscious ways by which these subjectivities are enjoyed (Hook, 2013; Malherbe, 2021a). It is within the context of struggle that we can forge the kinds of psychic and political connections required to tear away from those parts of ourselves that are not only complicit with neoliberalism's ideological mandate but that are unconsciously willed towards capitalist domination, including its racialised and gendered modes of oppression (Mbembe, 2019). An anti-capitalist psychology of community aims to assist activists in interrogating and re-symbolising neoliberal subjectivity precisely because class consciousness does not necessarily denote a decolonial unconscious. Yet, even though everyone experiences oppression differently under capitalism (which is not to say that we all experience it equally), the point of creating anti-capitalist subjectivities is to establish empathetic ways of relating to one another and the world so that we might work together, under a common experience of oppression, to change the world and, in so doing, change ourselves and our desires (Malherbe, 2021a). Once again, psychologists of community can set up therapeutic spaces wherein people can work with one another and on themselves to transform the (oftentimes repressed) neoliberal embeddedness within subjectivity and thus institute a revolutionary movement in subjectivity (see Parker, 2011).

Challenging and remaking subjectivity affords to us insight into how cultural ideals and norms become internalised and naturalised within and for individual subjects (Rutherford, 2018). We do not need to find solace within neoliberal ideologies that promise to alleviate contradiction through fantasies of hard work, the fetishised commodity, mastery and obedience, and/or repressive tolerance. We can, instead, see ourselves as *developing* subjects, with anti-capitalist action bringing about new fantasies of solidarity and modes of identification (Malherbe, 2021a). Indeed, people pass through a multitude of subjectivities when they resist capitalist oppression, many of which are formed against capitalism's particular identity-based oppressions. Therefore, to stress this point once more, an anti-capitalist psychology of community should not seek to arrive at *the* anti-capitalist subjectivity. Rather, psychologists of community can work with activists to grapple with the tensions and contradictions that come with building an anti-capitalist project that speaks to the material concerns of a multitude of subjectivities. In this, people do not reject identity as such, but work together to reject the violent ideological social processes that structure identification under neoliberalism, thereby transforming—and even revolutionising—how subjectivities are enjoyed and reproduced (see Rutherford, 2018). As such, the political concerns of the individual become fastened to and understood as part and parcel of those of the collective.

Recovering Cultural Memories

Under capitalism, cultural coloniality erases and/or territorialises those cultures which do not reflect the ideologies of capitalist modernity (Ratele, 2018). Cultural memory, in turn, can illuminate the ways by which colonial capitalism destroys, disfigures, and distorts subaltern histories (see Fanon, 1963). Put differently, remembering culturally can function as a kind of anti-capitalist re-symbolisation. However, articulating cultural memory for purposes of anti-capitalist conscientisation requires a basic understanding of two ideas: culture and memory. Let us begin by defining culture which—although a notoriously complex concept (Williams, 1977)—we can understand broadly as the shifting values, beliefs, practices, meanings, and norms of a social group or social groups (Reyes Cruz & Sonn, 2011). Culture, understood in this way, is always bound up with ideology and material existence, meaning that the form that culture assumes is determined by broader dynamics of power (Malherbe, 2020). Memory, on the other hand, can be defined—quite simply—as one's capacity to recall and store experiences and knowledge (Brockmeier, 2010). Memories are never beyond contestation, with the possibilities for remembering determined by dominant ideologies. Considering how these two terms operate together under the concept of cultural memory pushes psychologists of community to consider how memories are lodged, stored, and repressed within different cultures. Indeed, cultural memory denotes what is passed down and to whom. In Williams' (1977) formulation, cultural memory represents a kind of residual culture, whereby those cultural elements formed in the past are activated in the present in ways that can express new, anti-capitalist values and meanings (although this is not inevitable). If, with Amílcar Cabral (2016), we understand culture as the different ways-of-being in and moving through history, then cultural memories hold the potential to repair a sense of self and heal subjectivities by engaging with how capitalism obscures its own psycho-material impact. Such obscuratory practice includes systematically muting how slavery and colonialism live in and shape the present (i.e. coloniality), as well as repressing the political radicality of those decolonising anti-capitalist movements that are *willed towards community* (see Mbembe, 2021). Although he acknowledges that our ability to forget is important for psychological hygiene, Herbert Marcuse (1970) writes that "To forget is also to forgive what should not be forgiven if justice and freedom are to prevail … to forget past suffering is to forgive the forces that caused it without defeating those forces" (p. 185). Memories can thus be used to forge solidarities and develop an emancipatory consciousness in cultural climates that are structurally invested in forgetting (Watkins & Shulman, 2008). Through a visceral, collective knowledge of how capitalist conditions are established systematically, rather than via the meritocratic diligence of a few individuals, cultural memory offers a way into confronting neoliberal ideology's legitimation of brutality and violence.

It is because colonial capitalism underestimates the visceral power of culture that cultural memories are so important for re-symbolising neoliberal ideology (see Cabral, 2016). Such memories can illuminate—even if only partially—histories that have been distorted and ignored. People may then use these histories as an impetus for action. However, cultural memories do not retrieve history wholesale. They excavate, recover, recuperate, remake, and re-organise histories through contested, yet meaningful, signs (Bhabha, 1994). It is because cultural memories are not always activated through readily available symbols that an anti-capitalist psychology of community can be used to evoke memory in non-linguistic ways (e.g. through art or historical artefacts) that resist the flattening or making linear of memory (Gqola, 2010). This is what I refer to as cultural re-membering (see Malherbe, 2020), whereby people try to make sense of historical trauma by recovering their cultural identities and reconstructing dismembered pasts through radical narrative techniques that reject the kinds of linearity demanded by those historiographies which cohere with neoliberal ideology. Cultural re-membering can inform how psychologists work with communities to articulate, in a psychically appealing way, the demands of intergenerational justice as well as the emancipatory and oppressive components of capitalist history that neoliberal ideology has repressed and distorted (Mbembe & Rendall, 2002; Wright, 2019).

Cultures always include more than they consciously exclude (Said, 1993) and are characterised by a fundamental hybridity (Bhabha, 1994). Cultural memories represent a collective knowledge archive that cannot simply be recovered, wholesale, planned, and/or experienced in its totality (Cabral, 2016; Dutta, 2021; Eagleton, 2016). Cultural memories enable a telling of history through a multitude of fractured lenses that resist the ideological foreclosing or totalisation of history by allowing for a continuous breaking through of psychic truths (see Hook, 2013). The task of articulating cultural memory in meaningful ways is, therefore, exceedingly complex. Seeing to this complexity means that memory cannot be confined to a particular form. Psychologists of community should work with people to extract memories from a range of cultural understandings (which differ internally and borrow elements from one another), with the understanding that one can never return, entirely, to the kinds of dignity preserved within these memories. Yet, these memories are, themselves, a testament to people's ability to create culture in the face of capitalism's daily humiliations, disenfranchisements, and degradations (Cabral, 2016; Mbembe, 2021). Retrieving cultural memory uncovers, from the past, fragments of a socially just future. It is because these fragments are so psychically meaningful that they hold the potential to impel people to act (Malherbe, 2020), which is to say, to reject the oppressive consequences of history as inevitable by *working through* these consequences in an actional and reflective mode (see Hook, 2013). Resistance and solidarity can become especially transgressive and appeal to people in visceral and psychologically relevant ways when they are enacted through cultural registers that are attuned to the materiality of history (see Bhabha, 1994). As Walter Benjamin (2007) writes, the "struggling oppressed class itself is the depository of historical knowledge … the working class forget both its hatred and its spirit of sacrifice, for both are nourished by the image of enslaved ancestors rather than that of liberated grandchildren" (p. 260). Cultural memory may then present not only a way of sharing in common but also a democratically constructed way of understanding the psychological valances of capitalism (Eagleton, 2016). Psychologists can work with activists and other community members to democratically negotiate how tradition sits within contemporary struggles and, in so doing, articulate new styles of tradition that align with an anti-capitalist politics (see Malherbe, 2020).

The past appears not just in what we can recall but also in the very shape of our psychic processes, meaning that our psychological engagements with history (i.e. memory) are what we think and feel through (Pavón-Cuéllar, 2017). It is because cultural memories are fragmented that they cannot offer a coherent anti-capitalist political programme. Rather, the anti-capitalist potential of cultural memories lies in their "poetic instants", that is, those parts of memory that remind us that when life is free, fair, and just, it can be beautiful and worth living (Lehmann & Brinkmann, 2020). Cultural memories are central to developing non-ideological knowledges which are open to contradiction and formed through interactive and negotiable sociocultural practices of re-membering (see Brockmeier, 2010). For psychologists, working with people to recover cultural memories allows for an engagement with the psychic life of communities that is not always available through studious labour or archival work. It is with these psychic lives that communities can return to themselves through a collectively felt, non-linear historiography that is sensitive to the psycho-material particularities of capitalism (Said, 1993). Although the trauma of capitalism's long history cannot be overcome, through cultural memory, this trauma can be acknowledged and walked alongside (see Long, 2021), informing how people refuse the continuation of this history.

There are, of course, ways by which cultural memory can be drawn on to impose an oppressive, naturalised, and fetishised past. Aimé Césaire (1972) is well-aware of this when he advocates for anti-capitalism over a return to a mythic pre-capitalist epoch. Nonetheless, cultural memory can stretch the political imaginations of its participants, enabling them to learn from and reflect on how anti-capitalist struggle enters into contemporary culture and how neoliberal ideology seeks to expel it from culture (see Mbembe, 2019). It is because cultural memories can connect the histories of oppressed and oppressor that have been artificially separated (i.e. made to appear as differences rather than contradictions) by neoliberal ideology that these memories can foster powerful feelings of unity. When people take control of how their culture is re-membered, they exercise autonomy over the kinds of values that guide and lead political struggle (Ngũgĩ, 1993), thereby preserving the best of culture within contexts of struggle (Cabral, 2016). As Achille Mbembe (2021) writes, "We will have to learn to remember together, and, in so doing, to repair together the world's fabric and its visage" (p. 172). It is, therefore, because culture stores a version of the past within it that cultural memories can serve anti-capitalist purposes, which is to say that cultural memories can function as the building blocks for reconstructing community and paving the way for future-oriented action (Montero et al., 2017). It is in this way that cultural memories can re-establish the foundations of history so that we may draw upon this history in different, emancipatory ways (Hook, 2013).

While the cultural memories of the oppressed are not "right" or "wrong", they are real (Brockmeier, 2010), which makes them crucial not only for understanding capitalism's psycho-historical impact but also for activating future-oriented anti-capitalist energies. Cultural memories, we might say, hover over and even govern our relationship to the future, playing a part in how anti-capitalist efforts resist what Pumla Gqola (2010) calls unremembering, which is a calculated act of historical erasure that distorts and restrains collective consciousness (see also Dutta, 2021). It is imperative that an anti-capitalist psychology of community facilitate spaces wherein collectives can construct and re-symbolise those histories which push back against the organised unremembering inherent to neoliberal ideology (see Watkins & Shulman, 2008).

Art and the Popular Aesthetic

Under capitalism, political art, more often than not, functions as a commodity that services the ideological interests of the ruling classes by rendering the very act of seeing one of ownership and possession (Berger, 1972). Although art of this sort does not necessarily shy away from radical, anti-capitalist ideas, it tends to aestheticise these ideas, offering them as consumable spectacles to be witnessed rather than participated in (Sontag, 1977). As Chiara Bottici writes:

> The technical transformations of contemporary capitalism have tightened the link between politics and the [artistic] imaginal to such a degree that we can no longer ignore this fact. We have reached a critical threshold: the quantitative and qualitative changes to the imaginal are such that images are no longer what mediate our doing politics, but that which risks doing politics in our stead. (Bottici, 2014, p. 178)

A similar argument can be found in the work of Mark Fisher (2018), who demonstrates how art and popular culture can sublimate anti-capitalism by "doing" anti-capitalism for us (e.g. when watching a film with anti-capitalist motifs, those on the political Left might experience a kind of libidinal satisfaction that sublimates their dissident political energies). It is only when political art refuses to let the profit motive determine its form and content that it rejects neoliberalism's ideological hail (see Teo, 2017). Art of this sort is, however, usually short-lived because it is denied resources (Glăveanu, 2010).

Like culture, art is part of the Marxian superstructure. However, art remains distinct from culture (despite much culture eventually becoming art), with the latter revealing to us ways of knowing and being that are housed in the former (see Williams, 1961). Art is a conduit for cultural attitudes (Said, 1993) and thus holds much re-symbolisation potential. Indeed, art need not be the alienating, fetishised commodity that it becomes when hailed through the dictates of neoliberal ideology. It can, in fact, offer images that look beyond the capitalist social order. Art can also represent a creative process of communicating people's anti-capitalist ideas in ways that traverse the strictures of "rational" prose (Tanggaard, 2013). Considering all of this, and if re-symbolising efforts within an anti-capitalist psychology of community are to draw on the powerful and psychologically appealing potentialities of art, then art should not only be understood as a means through which to reveal the contradictions of neoliberal ideology. As a process and a product, art can also reflect the psycho-materiality of anti-capitalism in even more ambitious ways than concrete anti-capitalist political demands.

If we take seriously Raymond Williams' (1961) well-known assertion that culture is ordinary, then we can begin to think of art not as a singular work produced by a lone genius or an exceptional collective, but as a common practice of remaking the world that is, itself, always passing through an incomplete state of becoming (Tanggaard, 2013). In what Pierre Bourdieu (1984) calls the popular aesthetic, we are called upon to consider how art and everyday life can exist together. Bringing art into our day-to-day existence, he argued, speaks to a deeply humanistic need to participate in a world that, as the Marxists demonstrate, is produced by—but denied to—the majority. The popular aesthetic liberates freedom from neoliberal stricture and points to how freedom can denote the ability to create and to enjoy the creativity of others. A psychology of community has long engaged with artist collectives and the popular aesthetic (see Seedat et al., 2017; Watkins & Shulman, 2008). Society can be transformed to release and reflect the human potential for beauty, artistry, and creativity that is continually stifled under capitalism (Eagleton, 1976). These concerns should not drop out of an anti-capitalist psychology of community. Certainly, anti-capitalism cannot limit itself to the base material needs of survival. Aesthetic beauty should always form part of our psycho-political demands. As with anti-capitalist feminist struggles in the early twentieth century, ours is a struggle not only of bread but also of roses (Fraser et al., 2019). When we struggle against gentrification, for instance, we are not opposed to the construction of aesthetically pleasing neighbourhoods, but rather the fact that aesthetics is being determined and enjoyed by an elite few. An anti-capitalist psychology of community should seek to work with activists and other community members to ensure that a shared aesthetic is configured democratically, from below, and that it is not geared towards consumerism or capital investment. Activist work of this kind is, therefore, not only the concern of artists and aesthetes. It is a common struggle to live with beauty.

The popular aesthetic can inflect art with radical political content. Art of this kind "teaches us to see into things" (Benjamin, 2008, p. 255), to perceive our anti-capitalist politics in new ways (Berger, 1972). As Mbembe puts it, political art is always politicising art that is able:

> [T]o liberate the eye, to render it active and mobile, to set it in relation to manifold other psychic and physiological processes … The eye, in these conditions, is not a dead organ … its work is to explore what is missing: that is, to reconstruct, on the basis of multiple traces and indications, the object staged in the image - in short, to give rise to its appearing, to its coming alive. (Mbembe, 2021, p. 157)

It is this ability to see what is missing in neoliberal ideology's symbolic order that affords the artist (considered as anyone who creates, artistically) and audiences of art a truly spontaneous way of knowing (Fromm, 1942). While it would be inaccurate to say that art is knowledge in the traditional sense, art can grant to artists and audiences ways of knowing an experience of a situation (i.e. experiences of the self in the context of others) and thus extends our communicative capacities beyond the neoliberal ideological hail (see Eagleton, 1976). It is through imagination and reflection that art offers new ways of knowing, that is, a poetic knowledge that dreams and sees the future in the present, reflecting reality anew (Kelley, 2002). There is a humbling element to this kind of knowing. The silences within art, typically absent in linguistic information, call upon us to reflect deeply (see Berger, 1972) and engage with the kinds of otherness (including the Other within the self) that exists outside of the hegemonic binaries determined by neoliberal ideology (Dutta, 2021). At the same time, in what Said (1993) calls "the voyage in", art can assert the existence of those histories that colonial culture has sought to unremember and erase. In so doing, art can diminish the legitimacy of coloniality's attendant cultures. Urmitapa Dutta (2021), for example, argues that for many Miya communities, poetry is a central component for resisting coloniality's dehumanising master narratives. We might, then, say that through the creation of art, psychologists of community can work with anti-capitalist groups to confer new locations of importance (solidarity and marginalised histories, for instance, over competition and Eurocentrism) which code reality in ways that are unrealisable within the individualising perceptions and "whole" subjectivities offered by neoliberal ideology (Sontag, 1977; Williams, 1961).

With regard to the contradictions of capitalist ideology, art can make the familiar appear strange. Reflecting on that which we take for granted can reveal how capitalism is opposed to itself, rather than operating as a seamless whole. The playwright Bertolt Brecht refers to the artistic act of making strange as *Verfremdungseffekte* (or, the alienation effect), which can lead audiences to engage with the contradictory nodes within the familiar (Ezcurra, 2012). Through this kind of artistic dislocation that shocks people into new awareness, Brecht argued, audiences can move beyond politics as aesthetics—or spectacle—and towards actioning new, emancipatory sorts of familiarity (Eagleton, 1976). The point, then, is to connect the artistic re-symbolisation of the familiar with the kinds of organised anti-capitalist resistance discussed in Chap. 3. An excellent example of this is noted in the street art produced by the Ngamanye Amaxesha Collective in South Africa, which brings into public spaces the political demands of labour and student movements in the country (Malherbe, 2021a), thereby reclaiming public space by filling it with anti-capitalist content (see Teo, 2017). In this way, neoliberalism's ideological representations are, through the popular aesthetic, rendered illegitimate (Said, 1993). Although art cannot—in itself—change history, its ability to re-symbolise reality can serve as an active agent in catalysing our political imagination on which anti-capitalist change-making depends (Eagleton, 1976). Psychologists of community can work with groups to politicise the popular aesthetic's re-symbolising capacities by linking it with existing anti-capitalist resistance.

Bottici (2014) writes that "Politics is not (or no longer) a struggle for the distribution of power and the use of legitimate coercion, but has become increasingly a struggle for people's imagination" (p. 125). Art's relationship with the anti-capitalist political imagination is, however, not a straightforward one. Powerful political art can unsettle audiences by adhering to neoliberal ideology at one moment and challenging it at other moments. Such art can expose the limits of neoliberal ideology, and it can deliberately fail to transcend it (Eagleton, 1976). For those involved in an anti-capitalist psychology of community, art can assist people in grappling with the contradictions, regressions, and unspeakable aspects of an emancipatory ideal as it exists in reality. Political art can serve as a useful component of anti-capitalist struggle precisely because it does not look to fix the past or prefigure the future. Rather, it exposes the limitations of the present so that we might imagine into this present a more just and dignified way of living and being with one another. Art can politicise the imaginary by creating newness through a denial of the "facts" offered by neoliberal ideology (Bottici, 2014), pushing us to think through and act out a reality that is more just, but no less contradictory (Kornbluh, 2019). An anti-capitalist psychology of community should thus be concerned with political art and the popular aesthetic because each can facilitate nuanced ways of articulating the experience of suffering while holding contradiction within an anti-capitalist imaginary that looks to alleviate this suffering (Dutta, 2021).

Although art can offer commentary on the world, it is also part of the world's material composition (Sontag, 1977). Like all production under capitalism, the production of art (or, rather, profitable art) is part of the economic base (Eagleton, 1976) and in this sense points to oppressive or exploitative processes. These processes are obscured by neoliberalism's ideological celebration of the singular artistic genius or extraordinary artwork. As Benjamin (2008) writes, "The products of art and science owe their existence not merely to the effort of the great geniuses who created them, but also, in one degree or another, to the anonymous toil of their contemporaries" (p. 124). Yet, this alienating conception of artistic labour need not be accepted. Those involved with an anti-capitalist psychology of community can work together to create the conditions by which art is produced democratically and for its own sake, rather than for purposes of consumption and profit (Malherbe, 2020). It is in this respect that art can offer a living image of unalienated labour (see Eagleton, 1976), an image that can, in turn, inform and inspire demands for more equitable working conditions elsewhere. The revolutionary artist, according to Benjamin (2008), seeks to make equal various artistic productive forces and, in so doing, alters the relationship between artists and audiences, both of whom can become collaborators in the artistic process (Eagleton, 1976; Malherbe, 2020). Brecht, who I mentioned earlier, would often collaboratively rewrite his plays in light of how audiences reacted to them. His objective here was not only to emphasise the fact that society and individuals can be reassembled (Ezcurra, 2012) but also to accent the collective nature of artistic production (Eagleton, 1976). Dutta (2021), similarly, recounts that writing poetry has not been, for her, a solitary affair, but one that has enabled modes of connection, sharing, collective knowledge-making, and solidarity in the communities within which she works. It is in this respect that an anti-capitalist psychology of community should strive to enact a democratic process of producing art. Such a process should be accessible to all and should resist the relentless, meritocratic drive to reproduce capital (Teo, 2017).

An anti-capitalist psychology of community, in essence, conceives of art and the popular aesthetic through what Vlad Glăveanu (2010) calls the we-paradigm, whereby art is used by collectives to change the socio-political contexts in which art is embedded. Through common reference points, art can bring attention to how politics bears on the psychosocial subject in captivating ways all while serving as a cathartic catalyst for cultural memory (see McDonald et al., 2012). Without psychologising art or the popular aesthetic, psychologists of community can work with others to draw out the evocative power of art and artistic production to create new, anti-capitalist values that feel into experience while highlighting the contradictions that mark subjectivity, capitalism, and anti-capitalism (González Rey, 2016; Lehmann & Brinkmann, 2020).

Case Illustration: Committing Through Contradiction

In this section, I draw on the same participatory film project discussed in Chap. 3, wherein residents from Thembelihle, a low-income South Africa community, produced a documentary film titled *Thembelihle: Place of Hope*. However, because I was concerned with resisting the neoliberal political project in that chapter, I focused on how an anti-capitalist psychology of community could be used to strengthen anti-capitalist movements at public screenings of the documentary. The accent was, therefore, on the screening events and not the content of the documentary. Given my concern in the present chapter with resisting neoliberal ideology, I will focus here primarily on how the documentary itself informed anti-capitalist re-symbolisation.

To begin with, though, some context must be provided on xenophobic violence in Thembelihle and South Africa. Studies have consistently shown that xenophobic violence in post-1994 South Africa (concentrated almost exclusively in low-income areas in the country, Mngxitama, 2009) is a direct result of the desperation and frustration that has arisen from the unbearably high rates of unemployment and inequality, both of which are exacerbated by the State's adherence to neoliberal austerity (see Neocosmos, 2008; Seedat et al., 2010). Neoliberal ideology's focus on external differences over internal contradictions casts attention away from structural inequalities, with the poor, Black, foreign national made into a symbol of antagonistic difference, responsible for hundreds of years of capitalist colonial violence (Mngxitama, 2009). Xenophobic violence tends to erupt when the foreign Other is no longer *tolerated*. In Thembelihle, spates of xenophobic violence were noted in 2009 (Tselapedi & Dugard, 2013) and again in 2015 (Poplak, 2015). As one Ethiopian shop owner recounts in the documentary, during the 2015 attacks, the assailants "loot us ... beat us ... took everything from our shop … so it's very hard to recover at that time".

Xenophobic violence has always been a central concern for anti-capitalist movements in South Africa (Neocosmos, 2008), and Thembelihle is no different in this respect. Responding to the 2015 attacks, the Thembelihle Crisis Committee (TCC) offered protection to foreign nationals and later—in an effort to build cohesive social relations—co-hosted several friendly sports tournaments between nationals and foreign nationals in the community (Tselapedi & Dugard, 2013). It was for these efforts that the TCC and Thembelihle received the *Mkhaya Migrants Award: Most Integrated Community in South Africa* from the State's Department of Home Affairs (Department of Home Affairs, 2016). Yet, as is generally the case in South Africa, the manner by which TCC—as a grassroots organisation that espouses "socialism as its ideological compass in the struggle of shack dwellers" (Ngwane, 2021, p. 9)—curbed xenophobic violence in Thembelihle received no media coverage (Malherbe et al., 2021a) and was ignored by South Africa's politicians, some of whom have a record of actively endorsing xenophobic violence (Hayem, 2013; Neocosmos, 2008). This silence starkly contrasted with the extensive coverage that xenophobic violence in Thembelihle received in the South African media. When the success of grassroots efforts to fight xenophobia goes unreported in this way, xenophobic violence may be attributed, by some, to the nature of the poor national subject who enacts such violence and/or the character of the poor foreign national subjects who experience this violence (Duncan, 2016; Malherbe et al., 2021a). Resultantly, repressive State-led interventions into combatting violence in Thembelihle can be made to appear rational, just, and even necessary. The complicity of South Africa's media and its political elite in perpetuating xenophobic violence is, however, unsurprising when we concede that such violence stems from the neoliberal ideology to which both are committed.

By depicting how TCC sought to combat xenophobic violence (and the contradictions therein), the documentary sought to re-symbolise broader discourses around xenophobia in Thembelihle through the perspectives of foreign nationals who experienced such violence as well as TCC activists who worked with foreign nationals to curb this violence. At the time of the 2015 attacks, TCC was engaged in a protracted protest campaign for in situ development in Thembelihle. However, as one leader of TCC explains in the documentary, he and his comrades "had to suspend the protests because we were told that criminals were doing their own business [i.e., looting shops belonging to foreign nationals and beating foreign nationals]". He goes on to say that TCC "confiscated about 14 fridges [that looters had been taken from convenience stores owned by foreign nationals in Thembelihle]" and "took them back to our brothers and sisters from Africa". The struggles experienced by foreign nationals were, therefore, not perceived as external to the material struggles of the national residents of Thembelihle. These struggles were engaged as part of a general struggle against capitalism, which is significant in the context of South Africa, where the rights of foreign nationals are usually obscured in State policy and neglected by social movements (see Hayem, 2013; Malherbe et al., 2021b). TCC's anti-capitalist action attacked capitalism as a system of contradictions, rather than a society of differences, and in this reflected a new, radical humanism that rejected the divisive, partialised subjectivities that neoliberal ideology confers onto those who are Black, who are poor, and who are Other. TCC harnessed an actional language to re-symbolise its anti-capitalist politics and attune these politics to the concerns of the multitude who, despite their differential suffering, do not fit neoliberalism's ideological hail. In short, when the subjectivities hailed by TCC came to include the foreign national subjectivity, TCC's politics were expanded and made more inclusive.

At community screenings of the documentary, residents appeared to be moved by the insurgent, humanist project that TCC's anti-capitalist actions embodied. When one audience member, remarking on TCC's anti-xenophobic intervention, proclaimed "we are human beings, we are here!", nationals and foreign nationals in the audience responded with considerable applause. Many other audience members proclaimed that, despite living in Thembelihle for most of their lives, they were unaware that it was TCC that intervened in the xenophobic attacks and not the State. Similarly, they did not know of the award that their community had received for its anti-xenophobic action. Audiences grappled with how subjectivity could be built from the ground up and taken back from elite politicians who so often use humanist discourse to advance an agenda of neoliberal tolerance. Several audience members wanted to know more about how the community had fought xenophobia, while others shared their experiences of xenophobia. A number of young people also expressed their desire to become involved in the kind of organised anti-xenophobic action that had been captured in the documentary. As one young audience member declared, "I've lost hope in government ... Let's go back to us as a community". This, to my mind, expressed a desire to hail subjectivities via a belonging to an ethical community, rather than the illegitimate neoliberal ideology espoused by the South African State. Being was not, in other words, equated with having, as is the case with neoliberal ideology. Instead, individual being was expressed as being-with-others, wherein material and psychological needs were to be taken care of in a context of mutuality.

It is, however, important to stress that transforming subjectivities is an ongoing, critical task. To take back the subjective hail from neoliberal ideology and to construct the subject collectively—from below and through anti-capitalist political commitment—is to acknowledge that subjectivity is marked by contradiction and cannot offer the mythic security promised by the neoliberal subjective hail. An anti-capitalist psychology of community should seek to facilitate the kinds of reflection required to build resistance that is attentive to complex, fractured, and politicised subjectivities. Although TCC's attempts to advance a new, radical humanism were praised at the various screening events, audiences also critically assessed these efforts. Some took issue with how the agency of foreign nationals was, at times, diminished by TCC activists in the documentary (e.g. one activist implied that foreign nationals were effectively "saved" by TCC, while another's reference to foreign nationals as "our brothers and sisters from Africa" perpetuated the very discourse of South African exceptionalism through which much xenophobic sentiment in the country expresses itself; see Neocosmos, 2008). Audiences discussed with TCC activists the problems of an anti-capitalism that hailed the foreign national subject as perpetually wounded and/or victimised. Several audience members explicitly discussed the kind of agency that foreign nationals displayed when working with TCC to combat xenophobia in the community (e.g. during negotiations). Although some members of TCC proclaimed that these criticisms were undertaken in bad faith, others were more receptive, acknowledging that transforming subjectivities through anti-capitalist action is, indeed, a collective and ongoing project that requires participation from the multitude.

There were also moments in the documentary that revealed the contradictions inherent to the subjective hail of TCC's anti-capitalist politics. Where a TCC activist noted that xenophobic violence was enacted by "criminals" (i.e. distanced, othered subjects), one of the foreign nationals who spoke in the documentary was clear that some of these acts of violence were carried out by members of TCC: "whenever they protest, we are the targets. They directly come to our shop". Thus, for TCC, when one perpetuates xenophobic violence, that person is criminalised and denied TCC's anti-capitalist subjectivity. However, for foreign nationals, xenophobic violence was not incongruent with TCC's anti-capitalist subjectivity. Therefore, the experience of foreign nationals revealed the contradictions inherent to anti-capitalist action. In response to these contradictions, audiences at screening events engaged in critical discussions on how subjective belonging must attend to issues of unequal power, even in spaces where most subjects are, themselves, denied power. It was during these discussions that audiences addressed the kind of unconscious enjoyment that some of the members of TCC may have attained from "saving" foreign nationals. I attempted to facilitate these discussions in a way that did not condemn such enjoyment in a moralistic fashion, but acknowledged it and used it to highlight the importance of solidarity and political commitment—rather than individualising reward or satisfaction—as the drivers of anti-capitalist action. To transform neoliberal subjectivity through re-symbolisation is not to arrive at a neat resolution. Rather, questions of subjectivity are taken seriously so that, together, people can discern what subjectivity could mean in the context of building an anti-capitalist politics which reflects the interests of the multitude.

The documentary's re-symbolising engagement was not limited to transforming the subjective hail. The hybridity of cultural memory was also drawn on to articulate the contradictions of capitalism as well as anti-capitalism. This was clear in the documentary's depiction of a group of young people who described themselves as traditional dancers. This group, despite working and living in South Africa's Gauteng province, practised a form of dance that was traditionally performed in the KwaZulu-Natal province. By re-membering culture—as well as the memories locked into this culture—not through the static linguistic sign or with reference to pure origins, the dancers gave form to culture in a way that expressed its hybridity. The documentary was used by the dance group to showcase its work and bring the issue of culture into political conversations, thereby harnessing the psychic value of the past to understand and take action in the present.

At screening events, audiences discussed how support for cultural practice (and particularly those practices associated with cultures that have been brutalised, ignored, and/or disfigured by colonial capitalist ideology) should constitute an anti-capitalist demand by groups like TCC. As one TCC activist in the audience claimed, anti-capitalist groups must demand that the State "Sponsor culture! Culture plays a role in the economy. Culture starts from language. They [the State] must [support] language. They must support local wisdom and people must be developed. Government must provide them with financial assistance". It was because these cultures have been colonised, unremembered, and almost entirely erased that the very act of re-membering pointed to how anti-capitalism could appeal to people's psychic, cultural selves. Cultural memory, in this respect, served as the voyage into speaking about psychic wounding and how debasing one's common cultural identity has resulted, for many, in a loss of self. Although some audience members deployed rather static, utopian ideals of a lost culture, the hybridity of the dancers' cultural practices highlighted that perhaps the point was not to revive a comprehensive or monolithic culture, but to bring cultural memory into the present so that people could reckon with a traumatic past characterised by cultural erasure.

Although the documentary screenings allowed for some discussion among audiences on how anti-capitalist efforts should support artist collectives (and thus, freedom could denote the freedom to create, rather than the neoliberal freedom of individual responsibility), the documentary itself engaged the popular aesthetic in a somewhat different manner. During the process of participatory editing, community members maintained that shots of litter, sinkholes, potholes, and unpaved roads in

Thembelihle must feature prominently in the documentary in order to demonstrate that mere "service delivery" was not a sufficient characterisation of their anti-capitalist demands (see also Duncan, 2016). They were also calling for a beautiful community that reflected the popular aesthetic. As one activist in the documentary comments: "Thembelihle, for me, it's a community that lives together, that seems to say we want sanitation, we want water. I don't think that's a crime to ask that. It's not a crime. I want to, as a father, have a park where I will take my two beautiful daughters and feel like I'm part of the new South Africa". Connecting demands for the popular aesthetic (a park) to material demands (water, sanitation) stretches the anti-capitalist political imagination beyond just bread and butter issues, important as these issues are.

Audiences of the film further engaged the popular aesthetic at screening events. While most would argue that there is an art to making documentary films, whether these films constitute artistic products in and of themselves is perhaps debatable. However, I believe that documentaries like *Thembelihle: Place of Hope* can constitute art in that they provide a psycho-aesthetic form to life under capitalism and in this offer life as a kind of aesthetic (see Domenicali, 2017). Although life-as-art can be commodified and consumed in passive ways that align with neoliberal ideology, an aesthetic of this kind can also be used to highlight the contradictions of this ideology and to advance anti-capitalist action through aesthetic knowledge (which includes knowledge of the collective nature of aesthetic production). Therefore, myself and several of the community members who were involved in producing the documentary sought permission to screen it in various parts of Sandton, one of the most affluent municipalities in Johannesburg: "the heart of capitalism" as one TCC activist described it to me. We did so by projecting the documentary onto a large, mobile screen that was attached to a truck. Displaying the documentary in Sandown emphasised that the wealth of places like Sandton is made possible only through the underdevelopment of places like Thembelihle. As such, the screenings represented our attempt to harness the alienation effect to make clear the contradictions of capitalism which are routinely obscured by neoliberal ideology. A number of business-people in the area threatened to call the police and demanded that we cease screening the documentary. However, because we had received the necessary permissions, we refused to do so. At the same time, several low-paid people working in Sandton expressed considerable interest in the documentary. They spoke with TCC activists about the kinds of organised anti-capitalist struggles with which they were involved or wished to become involved. Using the documentary to produce the alienation effect, therefore, facilitated connections and solidarities across differently suffering subjects.

Those who watched the documentary harnessed an actional language that acknowledged the contradictions not only of capitalism but also of anti-capitalism. It was in this regard that people could embrace contradiction in ways that neoliberal ideology simply cannot. Put differently, connecting through an appreciation of difference was rejected, and instead attempts were made to forge solidarity through contradiction.

Conclusion

If we understand neoliberal ideology as naturalising capitalism's internal contradictions by making them appear to us as external differences that can be overcome with hard work or tolerance, then anti-capitalist re-symbolising efforts can be thought of as attempts to reveal the contradictions of capitalism: to name capitalist enemies so that their logic does not diminish, quell, or suffocate our emancipatory imagination. In this chapter, I have examined how an anti-capitalist psychology of community can be used to re-symbolise subjectivities, cultural memory, as well as art and the popular aesthetic. De-ideologisation work of this sort should not be made distinct from the kinds of organised political work discussed in Chap. 3. Indeed, de-ideologisation seeks to inform organised anti-capitalist action, shaping it and, in turn, being shaped by it. In this regard, an anti-capitalist psychology of community concerned with de-ideologisation strives always to stay with the material dimensions of ideology. Of course, there are many other ways by which an anti-capitalist psychology of community could be used for purposes of resisting neoliberal ideology. This chapter reflects my limited experience here. As with the previous chapter, my hope is that others will contribute to the development of what I am calling an anti-capitalist psychology of community by adding to, critiquing, and reformulating some of the nascent provocations that I have offered here.

References

Ailon, G. (2022). Profit, self, and agency: A reevaluation. *Critical Sociology, 48*(2), 251–264.
Balibar, E. (1995). *The philosophy of Marx*. Verso.
Benjamin, W. (2007). *Illuminations: Essays and reflections*. Random House.
Benjamin, W. (2008). *The work of art in the age of technological reproducibility and other writings on media*. Harvard University Press.
Berger, J. (1972). *Ways of seeing*. Penguin.
Bhabha, H. K. (1994). *The location of culture*. Routledge.
Bottici, C. (2014). *Imaginal politics: Images beyond imagination and the imaginary*. Columbia University Press.
Bourdieu, P. (1984). *Distinction: A social critique of the judgment of taste*. Harvard University Press.
Brockmeier, J. (2010). After the archive: Remapping memory. *Culture & Psychology, 16*(1), 5–35.
Cabral, A. (2016). *Resistance and decolonization*. Rowman & Littlefield International.
Césaire, A. (1972). *Discourse on colonialism*. Monthly Review Press.
Dean, J. (2019). *Comrade: An essay on political belonging*. Verso.
Domenicali, F. (2017). Life as an artwork: Étienne Souriau's aesthetics of existence. *Nouvelle Revue D'esthétique, 19*(1), 23–31.
Duncan, J. (2016). *Protest nation: The right to protest in South Africa*. University of KwaZulu-Natal Press.
Dutta, U. (2021). The politics and poetics of "fieldnotes": Decolonizing ethnographic knowing. *Qualitative Inquiry, 27*(5), 598–607.
Eagleton, T. (1976). *Marxism and literary criticism*. Methuen Co.
Eagleton, T. (2016). *Culture*. Yale University Press.

Ezcurra, M. P. (2012). On "shock": The artistic imagination of Benjamin and Brecht. *Contemporary aesthetics, 10*(1), 4.

Fanon, F. (1963). *The wretched of the earth.* Grove Press.

Fanon, F. (1967). *Black skin, white masks.* Grove Press.

Featherstone, D. (2012). *Solidarity: Hidden histories and geographies of internationalism.* Zed Books.

Fisher, M. (2018). *K-punk: The collected and unpublished writings of Mark Fisher (2004–2016).* Repeater Books.

Fraser, N., Arruzza, C., & Bhattacharya, T. (2019). *Feminism for the 99 percent: A manifesto.* Verso.

Fromm, E. (1942). *Fear of freedom.* Routledge.

Ghosh, J. (2021). Interpreting contemporary imperialism: Lessons from Samir Amin. *Review of African Political Economy, 48*(167), 8–14.

Glăveanu, V. P. (2010). Paradigms in the study of creativity: Introducing the perspective of cultural psychology. *New Ideas in Psychology, 28*(1), 79–93.

González Rey, F. (2016). Paths, development and discontinuity of some critical approaches to psychology in Latin America: What happened in that history? *Annual Review of Critical Psychology, 10*, 642–662.

Gqola, P. D. (2010). *What is slavery to me?* Wits University Press.

Hardt, M., & Negri, A. (2009). *Commonwealth.* Harvard University Press.

Hayem, J. (2013). From May 2008 to 2011: Xenophobic violence and national subjectivity in South Africa. *Journal of Southern African Studies, 39*(1), 77–97.

Holloway, J. (2010). *Crack capitalism.* Pluto Press.

Hook, D. (2013). *(Post)apartheid conditions: Psychoanalysis and social formation.* Palgrave Macmillan.

Jasko, K., Szastok, M., Grzymala-Moszczynska, J., Maj, M., & Kruglanski, A. W. (2019). Rebel with a cause: Personal significance from political activism predicts willingness to self-sacrifice. *Journal of Social Issues, 75*(1), 314–349.

Kelley, R. D. G. (2002). *Freedom dreams: The black radical imagination.* Beacon Press.

Kessi, S., & Boonzaier, F. (2018). Centre/ing decolonial feminist psychology in Africa. *South Africa Journal of Psychology, 48*(3), 299–309.

Kornbluh, A. (2019). *The order of forms: Realism, formalism, and social space.* The University of Chicago Press.

Lehmann, O. V., & Brinkmann, S. (2020). Revisiting "the art of being fragile": Why cultural psychology needs literature and poetry. *Culture & Psychology, 26*(3), 417–433.

Long, W. (2021). *Nation on the couch: Inside South Africa's mind.* Melinda Ferguson Books.

Malherbe, N. (2020). Articulating liberation psychologies of culture. *Journal of Theoretical and Philosophical Psychology, 40*(4), 203–218.

Malherbe, N. (2021a). A psychopolitical interpretation of de-alienation: Marxism, psychoanalysis, and liberation psychology. *Psychoanalysis, Culture & Society, 26*(3), 263–283.

Malherbe, N. (2021b). De-ideologization, liberation psychology, and the place of contradiction. *Journal for the Theory of Social Behaviour.* https://doi.org/10.1111/jtsb.12322

Malherbe, N., Seedat, M., & Suffla, S. (2021a). Analyzing discursive constructions of community in newspaper articles. *American Journal of Community Psychology, 67*(3–4), 433–446.

Malherbe, N., Seedat, M., & Suffla, S. (2021b). Understanding community violence: A critical realist framework for community psychology. *Journal of Community Psychology.* https://doi.org/10.1002/jcop.22660

Marcuse, H. (1970). *Eros and civilization: A philosophical inquiry into Freud.* Sphere Books.

Martín-Baró, I. (1994). *Writings for a liberation psychology.* Harvard University Press.

Marx, K. (1973). *Grundrisse.* Penguin.

Marx, K., & Engels, F. (1968). *Selected works.* Progress Publishers.

Mbembe, A. (2019). *Necropolitics.* Wits University Press.

Mbembe, A. (2021). *Out of the dark night: Essays on decolonization.* Wits University Press.

Mbembe, J. A., & Rendall, S. (2002). African modes of self-writing. *Public culture, 14*(1), 239–273.

McDonald, M., Catalani, C., & Minkler, M. (2012). Using the arts and new media in community organizing and community building: An overview and case study from post-Katrina new Orleans. In M. Minkler (Ed.), *Community organizing and community building for health and welfare* (pp. 288–304). Rutgers University Press.

McGowan, T. (2019). *Emancipation after Hegel: Achieving a contradictory revolution*. Columbia University Press.

Mngxitama, A. (2009). We are not all like that: Race, class and nation after apartheid. In S. Hassim, K. Tawana, & E. Worby (Eds.), *Go home or die here: Violence, xenophobia and the reinvention of difference* (pp. 189–205). Wits University Press.

Montero, M., Sonn, C. C., & Burton, M. (2017). Community psychology and liberation psychology: A creative synergy for an ethical and transformative praxis. In M. A. Bond, I. Serrano-García, C. B. Keys, & M. Shinn (Eds.), *APA handbook of community psychology* (Vol. 1, pp. 149–167). American Psychological Association.

Neocosmos, M. (2008). The politics of fear and the fear of politics: Reflections on xenophobic violence in South Africa. *Journal of Asian and African Studies, 43*(6), 586–594.

Ngũgĩ, W. T.'o. (1993). *Moving the Centre: The struggle for cultural freedoms*. James Currey.

Ngwane, T. (2021). *Amakomiti: Grassroots democracy in South African shack settlements*. Pluto Press.

Parker, I. (2011). *Lacanian psychoanalysis: Revolutions in subjectivity*. Routledge.

Pavón-Cuéllar, D. (2017). *Marxism and psychoanalysis: In or against psychology?* Routledge.

Poplak, R. (2015). *The army vs. Thembelihle: Where the truth lies*. Daily Maverick. https://www.dailymaverick.co.za/article/2015-05-05-the-army-vs-thembelihle-where-the-truth-lies/

Ratele, K. (2018). Toward cultural (African) psychology. In G. Jovanović, L. Allolio-Näcke, & C. Ratner (Eds.), *The challenges of cultural psychology: Historical legacies and future responsibilities* (pp. 250–267). Routledge.

Ratner, C. (2019). *Neoliberal psychology*. Springer.

Reyes Cruz, M., & Sonn, C. C. (2011). (De)colonizing culture in community psychology: Reflections from critical social science. *American Journal of Community Psychology, 47*, 203–214.

Rutherford, A. (2018). Feminism, psychology, and the gendering of neoliberal subjectivity: From critique to disruption. *Theory & Psychology, 28*(5), 619–644.

Said, E. W. (1993). *Culture and imperialism*. Random House.

Seedat, M., Bawa, U., & Ratele, K. (2010). Why the wretched kill in democratic South Africa: Reflections on rejuvenation and reconstruction. *Social Change, 40*(1), 15–27.

Seedat, M., Suffla, S., & Christie, D. J. (Eds.). (2017). *Emancipatory and participatory methodologies in peace, critical, and community psychology*. Springer.

Sontag, S. (1977). *On photography*. Dell.

Srnicek, N., & Williams, A. (2015). *Inventing the future: Postcapitalism and a world without work*. Verso.

Tanggaard, L. (2013). The sociomateriality of creativity in everyday life. *Culture & Psychology, 19*(1), 20–32.

Teo, T. (2017). Subjectivity, aesthetics, and the nexus of injustice: From traditional to street art. In S. H. Awad & B. Wagoner (Eds.), *Street art of resistance* (pp. 39–62). Palgrave Macmillan.

Teo, T. (2018). Homo neoliberalus: From personality to forms of subjectivity. *Theory & Psychology, 28*(5), 581–599.

Tselapedi, T., & Dugard, J. (2013). Reclaiming power: A case study of the Thembelihle crisis committee. *Good Governance Learning Network*. https://ggln.org.za/images/solg_reports/SoLG_2013.pdf#page=58

Watkins, M., & Shulman, H. (2008). *Toward psychologies of liberation*. Palgrave Macmillan.

Williams, R. (1961). *The long revolution*. Pelican.

Williams, R. (1977). *Marxism and literature*. Oxford University Press.

Wright, E. O. (2019). *How to be an anti-capitalist in the 21st century*. Verso.

Žižek, S. (2020). *A left that dares to speak its name: 34 untimely interventions*. Polity.

Chapter 5
Resisting Capitalist Rationality

In her feminist analysis of neoliberalism, Alexandra Rutherford insists that:

> One of the greatest challenges, perhaps, in "thinking a future" beyond neoliberalism is that it operates in and infuses the present in a particularly invisible and commonsense way. Unraveling the "common sense" of the present, then, becomes key to thinking the future differently. (Rutherford, 2018, p. 634)

In this chapter, I explore how those involved in an anti-capitalist psychology of community can take up the task of unravelling how neoliberal common sense—or what Wendy Brown (2015) refers to as neoliberal rationality—governs by economising and/or marketising almost all aspects of our lives, including conceptions of the human. This task, like that of resisting the neoliberal political economy (Chap. 3) and neoliberal ideology (Chap. 4), requires a materialist response that endeavours to understand neoliberal rationality so that we might loosen and eventually break its grip over our lives. Accordingly, I consider in this chapter what it is that an anti-capitalist psychology of community can offer to those who are engaged in articulating counter-hegemonic discourse, reconstituting the everyday, fighting for epistemic freedom, and fostering love and care.

It should be emphasised that I am not arguing for an anti-capitalist psychology of community that is, in any way, irrational. On the contrary, rationality is crucial for making anti-capitalism a viable, realistic, appealing, and common-sense concern (see Holloway, 2010). The fact that rationality can (and, when placed within a neoliberal frame, does) imply one's duty to maintaining an oppressive status quo should not overshadow how rationality can be made into a rebellious force that breaks through the economising parochialism and constant spectacle that characterises neoliberalism (Hardt & Negri, 2009). Even when we cannot make the world more rational, we can make the rational more worldly (Wark, 2020). We demonise rationality as such at our peril, and we should strive to pry it from neoliberalism so that we can remake it in the image of anti-capitalist emancipation. Therefore, I insist in this chapter that an anti-capitalist psychology of community looks to establish a new rationality, or humanising frame, with which to build and understand the world and the psychosocial subjects who make and are made by this world. A new rationality of this sort is fundamental, I argue, for establishing the values which sustain a commitment to anti-capitalist struggle and that serve as the benchmark by which to assess this commitment (see Wright, 2019).

N. Malherbe, *For an Anti-capitalist Psychology of Community*, Community Psychology, https://doi.org/10.1007/978-3-030-99696-3_5

Counter-Hegemony and Questions of Discourse

Although discourse has been theorised in several, sometimes conflicting, ways (see, e.g. Fairclough, 2003; Foucault, 1971; Laclau & Mouffe, 1985; Potter & Wetherell, 1987), it can be understood, broadly, as the different discursive practices involved in constructing knowledges and their legitimacy (Hall, 1997). Something only becomes meaningful to us once it has been connected to a discursive identity of some kind (De Cleen et al., 2021). However, discursive identities are never fixed. They are subject to revision, adaptation, and even erasure. Attempts to fix the meaning of discourse tell us about the functioning of dominant neoliberal rationalities (Torfing, 2005). Those who lack socioeconomic power have very little influence over the oppressive, narrow, and/or stereotypically informed discourses by which they are most often constructed (Tigar, 2009), and as such, most people are not formed or depicted by discourses of their own making (Rappaport, 1995). For instance, the coloniser names the colonised in order to fix onto the colonised an essence against which the coloniser's fixed, superior, essence can be defined (Mbembe, 2001). Today, capital shapes a society's dominant discursive apparatuses, ensuring that people are understood through an economising rationality which may be deployed through biopolitics, psychopolitics, and/or necropolitics. These struggles over discursive fixity can, however, represent fertile ground for anti-capitalist struggles over rationality.

Dominant discourses are not monolithic or homogenous. Rather, they are hegemonic. Hegemony, Gramsci (1971) teaches us, is achieved via people's consent (which can be active but is, due to a lack of viable alternatives, more often passive, Chibber, 2022), rather than through overt dominance. Necropolitical hegemonic discourses press into us images of who is legitimate, who is deviant, who is Other, and who should or should not be "reasonably" allowed to exist (see Mbembe, 2019). Discursive hegemony, in other words, determines how worth and meaning are conferred in a society. For neoliberal rationality, this means attaching social value to the economic and very little else, effectively rendering the economic a master code (see Mbembe, 2001). It is through biopolitical hegemony, though, that we conform, bodily, to the dictates of neoliberal rationality and through psychopolitical hegemony that such rationality determines the legitimacy of our feelings. At the same time, these attempts to fix the meaning of hegemonic discourse can reveal the weaknesses of hegemony precisely because a stabilised discourse fails to capture the movements and shifts of meaning within a given discursive field (see Torfing, 2005). We can delegitimise hegemonic discourse—and the grip that neoliberal rationality holds over hegemony—by looking to the limits of such discourse, examining what it excludes so that we can discern what is most threatening to its internal logic (Laclau & Mouffe, 1985). This is important for anti-capitalism because when neoliberal hegemonic discourse is confronted with new events that it cannot convincingly explain, represent, signify, or domesticate, the discursive terrain is pried open for struggles to offer new, more rational, anti-capitalist political projects with which people can identify (Torfing, 2005). These efforts to challenge hegemony and replace it with new modes of rationality—which are known as counter-hegemonies—tend to be gradual. Gramsci (1971) spoke of counter-hegemonies as enacting a "war of position", where protracted, incremental cultural, and political action challenges and erodes oppressive social systems from within, slowly breaking down their ideological elements and clearing the way for more radical, insurrectional social change (see Torfing, 2005), which he called the "war of manoeuvre". It is, therefore, through the counter-hegemonic war of position that we can begin the process of wresting rationality away from the capitalist class (Hardt & Negri, 2009).

Psychologists of community who work with people to enhance counter-hegemonic strategies that reject neoliberalism's economising rationality cannot do so without a sound understanding of how capitalist hegemony functions, not least of all because counter-hegemonic insurgency is often subtly denuded and recuperated through hegemonic frames of meaning (e.g. the way that mainstream news coverage of anti-capitalist protest action tends to focus on whether such action is legitimate, rather than questioning the legitimacy of the capitalist system to which such protest is directed; see Malherbe, Seedat, & Suffla, 2021). Yet, psychologists of community must also examine how hegemonic discourse is wielded outside of dominant centres of power. Counter-hegemonic action should concern itself not only with how communities are legitimised, denied, and/or Othered by hegemonic discourses (whether this is at the biopolitical, psychopolitical, or necropolitical level) but also with how hegemonic discourse is reproduced at the level of community. Psychologists of community and those with whom they work should remain attuned to what is included and excluded from conceptions of community and what this says about advancing inclusive anti-capitalist counter-hegemonies (i.e. new rationalities) across communities (see Torfing, 2005).

Inter-community conflict is, of course, rife when seeking to build counter-hegemonies within community contexts. There are always competing discourses tussling for hegemony (as well as for counter-hegemonic potency) within any community setting (see, e.g. Cornell et al., 2020). The task of an anti-capitalist psychology of community is to build links between and across these different discourses, creating space for people to hold and engage tensions while moving forward with these tensions instead of becoming politically debilitated by them. It is thus through, rather than despite, tensions that psychologists of community can work with people to develop anti-capitalist counter-hegemonies. Embracing tensions (or what I prefer to call contradictions; see Chap. 1) guards against locking antagonistic community actors into their discursive locations in a way that forecloses dialogue, critical reflection, and solidarity-making (Cornell et al., 2020). If, indeed, a "community is formed and re-formed every time its history is told" (Poks, 2015, p. 66), then producing counter-hegemonies through tension can allow for the formation of a community where the universal is not an exclusionary concept, but rather "implies a relation of inclusion in some already existing thing or entity … It presupposes a relation of belonging between multiple singularities" (Mbembe, 2021, p. 110). Universalising counter-hegemonies of this sort strive towards a material and psychological wellbeing based on the humanistic injunction that all communities contain within them pluriversality.

Speaking to the difficulties of building counter-hegemonies through tension, Laclau and Mouffe (1985) propose that, far from a synthesised, monolith, or a simple united front, counter-hegemonic struggles are able to bring different struggles together through empty signifiers (i.e. signifiers without definitive signifieds) that resist fixed meaning. Empty signifiers (which could include words like "democracy", "socialism", or "community") do not lie dormant or oppose meaning in ways that foster political inertia. Their power lies in the fact that, because their meanings are not fixed, they can be continually reconstituted through a new rationality that is, itself, determined by a democratically negotiated anti-capitalist politics that moves with the emancipatory demands of the moment. When anti-capitalism is not bound to fixed labels, it can transgress the limitations of these labels (Holloway, 2010). It is in this sense that anti-capitalism can become a community-led counter-hegemonic imperative that rejects stagnant neoliberal rationality and the non-relational subjective fixity of homo economicus. Establishing counter-hegemony through empty signifiers recognises that meaning is negotiated through an antagonistic, politically committed multitude (Hardt & Negri, 2009) and establishes new possibilities for rationality by disturbing supposedly fixed meaning (Rutherford, 2018). For those involved in an anti-capitalist psychology of community, attempts to construct counter-hegemony via empty signifiers can foster attentiveness to changes in social consciousness, discursive contradiction, and movements of meaning within struggle, thereby opening up space for activists' learning and reflection (see Collins, 2003).

When psychologists work with communities to build counter-hegemony, they are attempting to exert pressure on neoliberalism's governing rationality and engage in a kind of historiographical re-appraisal of social value that looks to pry rationality away from neoliberalism's discursive coordinates (see Collins, 2003). By struggling together to build an anti-capitalist politics through empty signifiers, we disregard the supposedly totalising explanatory power of hegemonic discourse. In this, we can offer new emancipatory horizons that do not attempt to replace neoliberalism with a differently oppressive discursive totality. Counter-hegemony is, therefore, always actional. Although that which escapes meaning within hegemonic discourse sets the conditions for counter-hegemony, we can only seize upon these conditions with political action that offers and demands support for alternatives to neoliberal rationality (see Saad-Filho, 2017). As such, no war of position should be undertaken without an eye on the war of manoeuvre (see Gramsci, 1971). It is perhaps because of the action orientation of anti-capitalist counter-hegemony, with its militant insistence on a more egalitarian rationality, that Boaventura de Sousa Santos (2016) understands counter-hegemony as representative of an insurgent cosmopolitanism.

The Everyday

Paul Harrison (2000) provides a useful definition of the everyday. He describes it as the very close, familiar, and dynamic experiences of people's day-to-day lives which shape their identities and form the unnoticed background of their perceptions.

A concern with the everyday is a concern for the life-world, that is, the daily living and common sense that quietly influences how people live with one another (see Montero et al., 2017). The everyday tends to go unannounced, which is how it exerts power over our lives and why it is difficult to study or understand (Johansson & Vinthagen, 2020). When we approach neoliberalism as a normative rationality, we are effectively interested in the neoliberal everyday. The manner by which neoliberal rationality informs the everyday (e.g. how we speak, move, know, dress, sense, and be) points towards the systemic functioning of neoliberalism (Suffla et al., 2020). Taking a biopolitical frame, we see the neoliberal everyday influencing how we move and interact in accordance with the profit motive. If, however, we assume a psychopolitical frame, we can see the ways by which neoliberal rationality appeals to our psychology within day-to-day settings (e.g. through advertising, commodities, social media). A necropolitical frame will then raise several other questions when we consider the neoliberal everyday, such as how:

> does one live when the time to die has passed, when it is even forbidden to be alive, in what might be called an experience of living the 'wrong way round'? How, in such circumstances, does one experience not only the everyday but the hic et nunc when, every day, one has both to expect anything and to live in expectation of something that has not yet been realized, is delaying being realized, is constantly unaccomplished and elusive? (Mbembe, 2001, p. 201)

No matter what frame we assume though, it is through the subject as a psycho-material body that neoliberal rationality governs at the level of the everyday.

The everyday is not all-determining. In what is called everyday resistance, people act into the everyday to undermine oppressive powers and in so doing create new rationalities (Johansson & Vinthagen, 2020; Montero et al., 2017; Scott, 1985). Everyday resistance speaks to subordinated people's creative and innovative actions which reject the situation in which they find themselves. In his anthropological work with Malaysian workers, James C. Scott (1985) found many forms of everyday resistance, including refusals, go-slows, evasions, false compliance, sarcasm, disloyalty, passivity, theft, pilfering, mocking, satire, sabotage, disruptions, and feigned ignorance. These forms of resistance tend to be invisible to elites. As such, everyday resistance is crucial for survival, especially in contexts where overt anti-capitalist resistance is too risky (Johansson & Vinthagen, 2020). At the same time, not every single act of refusal can be considered everyday resistance. We should understand everyday resistance as those actions which are undertaken routinely but are not necessarily articulated or formally organised. In this regard, everyday acts of resistance can only be understood in relation to the powers that they are acting against. Therefore, if an action is to be considered an act of everyday resistance, it must at least have the potential to influence and change dominant patterns of power (Johansson & Vinthagen, 2020).

The everyday is an under-considered site of anti-capitalist politics (Rosales & Langhout, 2020) and represents what is sometimes referred to as "infrapolitics" (see Scott, 1989). As such, it is "through the everyday that we feel politics" (Suffla et al., 2020, p. 348). Although anti-capitalist everyday activity does not always have long-term consequences, it illuminates a different world, a world that was created by people. This leaves an impression that can last for a long time (Holloway, 2010). An anti-capitalist psychology of community is tasked with actioning this powerful impression by working with people to make visible the anti-capitalist valances of their everyday activity so that the everyday might be altogether altered. As Henri Lefebvre (2002) argues, "To change the everyday is to bring its confusions into the light of day and into language; it is to make its latent conflicts apparent, and thus to burst them asunder. It is, therefore, both theory and practice, critique and action" (p. 226). In working to annunciate everyday anti-capitalist resistance (see Suffla et al., 2020), an anti-capitalist psychology of community can contribute to making anti-capitalism a rational mode of common sense, ensuring that resisting neoliberal rationality is not associated with deviance, but with a shared ethics or regard for a non-economised life (see Cabral, 2016). Moreover, locating and announcing everyday resistance can point towards and symbolise people's anti-capitalist desires and actions which can, in turn, strengthen their commitment to a collective anti-capitalist politics (see Malherbe, Ratele, et al., 2021). Yet, because the everyday, by definition, always hides from plain sight, psychologists of community may need alternative or new methods to uncover everyday resistance in places that are not always considered by psychology's Eurocentric knowledge-making frames (Suffla et al., 2020; Trott, 2016).

It would be too didactic to claim that within the everyday we find either neoliberal oppression or anti-capitalist resistance. At different moments, the everyday can be one, the other, both, or neither (see Lefebvre, 2002). An anti-capitalist psychology of community should, therefore, aim to work with people to identify and aggrandise anti-capitalist meanings, forms, and styles within the everyday (Harrison, 2000) and/or articulate interventions within the everyday that seek to de-link the everyday from neoliberalism's dehumanising rationality. Collectively identifying and changing the everyday in these ways may then serve to attune people to how others in their community resist capitalism. Certainly, making connections between these different resistances can assist us in seeing, thinking, and being outside of neoliberal rationality's seemingly all-pervasive purview. As Srnicek and Williams (2015) assert, everyday anti-capitalist activities "make global capitalism small enough to be thinkable" (p. 15), and, when considered together, these activities can project images—even if only partial, temporary, incomplete, and fragmented—of a life beyond capitalist relations of production (see Hardt & Negri, 2009). As such, people may wish to work together to pursue and make viable an exodus from capitalism and its rationalities. An anti-capitalist psychology of community must make itself of use to the ways that people envision and enact this exodus.

Everyday resistance can highlight how people are reclaiming, within their everyday lives, the dignity that is being erased under neoliberal rationality. Such small, infrapolitical reclamations can then be channelled and reflected in the grander, more ambitious demands of organised anti-capitalist movements (see Malherbe, Ratele, et al., 2021). People can, in this way, build coalitions between their everyday lives, reproduction, relations to nature, labour, social relations, organisational forms, mental conceptions, institutions, and other spheres of life that are segregated and individualised when conceived of through neoliberal rationality (see Harvey, 2017).

Psychologists of community can, therefore, work with people to articulate everyday resistance in ways that inform the kinds of organised anti-capitalist resistance examined in Chap. 3.

Although everyday resistance can strengthen organised anti-capitalist movements (Johansson & Vinthagen, 2020), this should not diminish the importance of everyday resistance in and of itself (Rosales & Langhout, 2020). Resisting neoliberal rationality within the everyday may be the most viable, safe, and appealing mode of anti-capitalism for many people, especially those for whom life under capitalism is so precarious, such as migrant labourers. As Srnicek and Williams (2015) claim, "The event (as revolutionary rupture) becomes an expression of the desire for novelty without responsibility. The messianic event promises to shatter our stagnant world and bring us to a new stage of history, conveniently voided of the difficult work that is politics" (p. 177). Or, as Scott (1989) argues, to proclaim that "'real resistance' is organized, principled, and has revolutionary implications ... overlook[s] entirely the vital role of power relations in constraining forms of resistance" (p. 51). By looking to those everyday anti-capitalist resistance efforts which find expression in de-centred plurality and that address several different dominant powers at once, psychologists of community can engage with anti-capitalism beyond the spectacle of movements (Johansson & Vinthagen, 2020). Accordingly, an anti-capitalist psychology of community must attune itself to the vast spectrum of anti-capitalisms. Rather than always prioritising one anti-capitalist approach over others, we can make connections between different approaches all while remaining sensitive to the sorts of unequal power dynamics that have ensured the fracturing of anti-capitalisms in the first place.

Johansson and Vinthagen (2020) argue that lifestyles, like veganism, can also constitute a form of everyday resistance. If these ways of life enter into culture, as veganism has in some places, they can form a kind of everyday counter-hegemony. In this sense, everyday resistance can go beyond dominant neoliberal rationality, creating other ways of life through repetition. For the purposes of an anti-capitalist psychology of community though, I wish to note a particular kind of anti-capitalist way of life which is known as prefiguration. Prefiguration, or prefigurative politics as it is sometimes called, denotes the actualisation of a post-capitalist life now, within the neoliberal present (Carroll, 2009). Emancipation is, in this way, prefigured in the here-and-now (Srnicek & Williams, 2015), with the irrational nature of neoliberal rationality exposed by offering a new, more rational way of being in the world, even if this is limited by capitalist social arrangements. As Samir Amin (2014) writes: "the construction of the future, even if it is far off, starts today" (p. 133). Prefiguration can alter micro-relations and, in turn, influence macro-structures. In this regard, prefiguration has the potential to move anti-capitalist politics beyond protest demands and towards new ways of living (Trott, 2016). John Holloway succinctly formulates this when he proclaims that:

> The real determinant of society is hidden behind the state and the economy: it is the way in which our everyday activity is organised, the subordination of our doing to the dictates of abstract labour, that is, of value, money, profit. It is this abstraction which is, after all, the very existence of the state. If we want to change society, we must stop the subordination of our activity to abstract labour, do something else. (Holloway, 2010, p. 133)

In doing something else, the micro comes to impact the macro in important ways. We can see an example of this in what Erik Olin Wright (2019) calls the social and solidarity economy, whereby economic activities and community organisations are structured in ways that embody egalitarian, solidaristic values that reflect the needs of people rather than the profit motive (e.g. community gardens, free clinics, recycling initiatives, public art). Through these prefigurative everyday anti-capitalist initiatives, people can begin to realise and take back the common (Hardt & Negri, 2017). Part of an anti-capitalist psychology of community's concern with the everyday is to work with people to build connections between these sorts of anti-capitalism that already exist in people's work lives, private lives, and social lives. In this, people can, together, develop a vision of anti-capitalism whose appeal lies in the fact that it is already being realised.

Community is central to how we engage with the everyday. Where formalised anti-capitalist movements rely on the solidarity relation (see Chap. 3), the everyday denotes a concern with community-based micro-alternatives which escape capitalism, sometimes just momentarily (see Wright, 2019). Under neoliberal rationality, a community's everyday reproduction depends on money, and in this sense, the economic "does indeed become the community; but a community empty of moral passion or of humane meanings" (Harvey, 2017 p. 168). The anti-capitalist everyday seeks to create a common, humanising, pluriversal community (a "world of many worlds" as the Zapatista slogan has it, Holloway, 2010), whereby several alternatives are proposed that confront neoliberal rationality and render it manageable so that we can move past it (Srnicek & Williams, 2015). It is, therefore, in the everyday that people can locate those elements of radical democracy that neoliberal rationality has sought to undermine, and as such, the everyday can bring into focus a particular kind of community-embedded, egalitarian anti-capitalism that lies beyond the focus of most anti-capitalist movements (see Amin, 2014). Indeed, it is within the everyday, rather than protest (important as protest is), that people create worlds beyond capitalism (Holloway, 2010). Psychologists of community whose work is concerned with building anti-capitalism cannot ignore how anti-capitalism already exists in people's daily community-making activity. As such, these psychologists are challenged to work with people to create links between everyday anti-capitalist activity so that people can, together, make even bigger the anti-capitalist worlds that they have—on a small, fractured scale—already created. When psychologists of community focus on the anti-capitalist everyday, a mode of collective agency comes into view that alters our perspective of struggle: it is not people who struggle against neoliberal rationality, but rather neoliberal rationality that must struggle against the insurgency of people's humanity as it is expressed in the everyday (Holloway, 2010).

Epistemic Freedom

The history of knowledge is one that tells us more about power than it does about truth (Medina, 2011), with advances in science oftentimes denoting advances in capitalist regulation and control (De Sousa Santos, 2016). Under capitalism, the most rewarded knowledges tend to be those that service capital in some way (Amin, 2014). Consequently, the knowledges which are deemed legitimate and that receive the resources required to survive are usually those which cohere with neoliberal rationality. This has implications for the knowledge-making enterprise, which is known as epistemology. When considered through neoliberal rationality, knowledge production appears to be the vocation of select individuals (oftentimes seen as lone geniuses; homo economicus *par excellence*) who may use knowledge for the social good as long as this knowledge does not disrupt the flow of capital. Moreover, neo-liberal rationality also influences the material process of knowledge production. The individualising and economising forces of neoliberal rationality come up against what Marx (1973) called "the general productive forces of the social brain" (p. 693), or the "general intellect", which are the collective social knowledges that serve as the basis for production. Under capitalism, the general intellect gets congealed into fixed capital (i.e. machines, or what Marx called "dead labour") which, in turn, ensures the exploitation of the labour force (Wark, 2017, 2020). Thus, it is not only the content of knowledge or how knowledge is used that comes to reflect neoliberal rationality. We also see the influence of neoliberal rationality in how knowledge is produced.

When epistemology is subject to neoliberal rationality, various forms of political control are made possible. Today, the proliferation of the Internet and online activity more generally has meant that corporations are granted unprecedented access to people's data. These data constitute knowledge when they are used by States and/or corporations to exercise biopolitical and psychopolitical control, as was the case in the 2018 Facebook-Cambridge Analytica data scandal (see Zuboff, 2019). Regarding necropolitics, because epistemology is so closely linked to ontology (i.e. ways of being in the world), to delegitimise knowledge is also to delegitimise the lives which produce this knowledge. As such, epistemicide (the near-total destruction of knowledge, de Sousa Santos, 2016) and epistemic violence (the harmful and inaccurate representation of the Other, Spivak, 1988) are regularly deployed in the name of neoliberal rationality to erase the interiority and humanity of the peoples associated with particular knowledges, rendering them little more than a "body-thing" that exists apart from considerations of the human (Mbembe, 2001, p. 27). It is thus through necropolitics that neoliberal rationality effectively asserts traditional morality over knowledge-making all while justifying the expansion of the neoliberal project through extractive systems of coloniality (see Ndlovu-Gatsheni, 2018).

Although several psychologists involved in mainstream community engagement have perpetuated epistemic violence as well as—albeit to a lesser degree—epistemicide, there are those practising a psychology of community, especially those influenced by the so-called decolonial turn in the discipline, who have sought to enact what Sabelo Ndlovu-Gatsheni (2018) calls epistemic freedom, a practice which insists on the right to interpret the world from where one stands and, in so doing, liberates rationality from coloniality and neoliberal metrics (Malherbe et al., 2022; Ratele, 2019). Honouring epistemic freedom can facilitate knowledge-making that connects the common with the ordinary and the labouring with the playful while—at the same time—making clear that how we know, collectively, influences the objects of our knowledge (see Wark, 2020). Epistemic freedom thus offers us visions of disclosing the world that are quite removed from neoliberal rationality's conception of freedom as market discipline (see Mbembe, 2021).

   The fight for epistemic freedom calls upon psychologists of community and those with whom they work to reject the utilitarianism, self-promotion, self-mastery, and hermeneutics of the self that characterise homo economicus (Teo, 2018; also see Chap. 2). As such, a psychology of community must go beyond the strictures of linearity demanded by Enlightenment by privileging forms of knowledge-making that are unlikely to cohere with the consumable knowledge products demanded by neoliberal rationality (see Poks, 2015; Seedat & Suffla, 2017; Smith, 2021). In other words, psychologists of community should engage knowledges and sites of epistemological production that have been rejected, maimed, or destroyed by the epistemological mechanisms of neoliberal rationality. Here, Maritza Montero et al. (2017) stress that the episteme should be approached by psychologists of community as a general mode of knowing (a mode which, I would add, is indicative of a particular production process): a sort of tacit knowledge that informs how people engage with one another and their communities. Psychologists of community who work with people to create the material conditions required for epistemic freedom, and to de-link knowledge-making from a stifling neoliberal rationality, are not attempting to produce new knowledge. Rather, they strive to honour subaltern knowledges that have been subject to epistemic violence and epistemicide and to make it clear that neoliberal rationality's systematic delegitimisation of these knowledges makes the very existence of such knowledges—and the fight for their survival—matters of anti-capitalism. Exercising epistemic freedom may not necessarily give form to explicitly anti-capitalist knowledge, but it does highlight and reject neoliberal rationality's dehumanising grip over the production and maintenance of subaltern knowledge (see Spivak, 1988).
   Epistemic freedom can be harnessed in explicitly political ways. Psychologists of community can work with activists to promote and develop a relevant political vocabulary that is alive to the most pertinent anti-capitalist concerns and that rejects the dominance that neoliberal semiotics holds over rational perception. Although a vocabulary of this sort may rely on neologisms and local knowledges (sometimes both at once, interpreting established knowledge traditions through the new), it can also rely on *détournement*, which refers to taking back vocabularies from capitalism via an emancipatory inversion of meaning (see Debord, 1977). For instance, when situated within neoliberal rationality, the words "diversity", "democracy", and "entrepreneur", respectively, imply liberalism, imperialism, and profit-making. Yet, when placed within a new register grounded in anti-capitalist epistemic freedom, these same words can denote creativity, collectivity, and fairness (see Hardt & Negri, 2017). In short, exercising epistemic freedom to politicise what and how we know contributes to what Amílcar Cabral (2016) called a culture of learning which can reach far beyond anti-capitalist collectives while, at the same time, rendering the politics of these anti-capitalist collectives more rational than neoliberalism.
   An anti-capitalist psychology of community can draw on its institutional embeddedness for the resources and tools required to exercise epistemic freedom (a task which is oftentimes undertaken with participatory action research methodologies; see Lazarus, 2018) and in the process use these resources against the very political

economy that availed them in the first place. The point, then, becomes not just to speak different knowledges, but to fight for the material conditions necessary for epistemic freedom (e.g. apparatuses for articulating knowledges; knowledge communications; and the time required to think, write, speak, and develop knowledge). It is only through these conditions that subaltern knowledges can begin to accrue the legitimacy that has been denied to them by neoliberal rationality. As Hardt and Negri (2000) insist: "Truth will not make us free, but taking control of the production of truth will. Mobility and hybridity are not liberatory, but taking control of the production of mobility and stasis, purities and mixtures is" (p. 156).

Establishing epistemic freedom—as well as making clear the anti-capitalist valances of epistemic freedom—is, of course, not without contradiction. An anti-capitalist psychology of community might, therefore, make use of what José Medina (2011) calls epistemic friction, or the contestation to which knowledge-making must be subjected if it is to integrate epistemic exclusions, counter-hegemonies, and disqualifications into its purview. When forged through epistemic friction, we guard against epistemic freedom being made into a regulatory practice (see De Sousa Santos, 2016). Instead, it becomes a matter of continuous contestation and commitment, both of which push psychologists of community and those with whom they work to embrace contradiction within an anti-capitalist politics that is attentive to the material requirements of epistemic freedom (see Chap. 2).

Although to know is always only to know partially (Wark, 2020), an anti-capitalist psychology of community's concern with epistemic freedom is about political commitment rather than liberal permissiveness (see Wark, 2017), and in this very particular sense, it is a psychology concerned with truth, albeit the kinds of truth that neoliberal rationality's economising truth regimes represent as lies, if they represent them at all (see Brown, 2015). Working with the oppressed to advance epistemic freedom allows for the truths of capitalist exploitation to emerge, truths which anti-capitalist political programmes cannot ignore if they are to retain legitimacy and popular support (Harvey, 2020). Anti-capitalist tactics can work to advance an insurrection of subjugated knowledges (Medina, 2011) and build these knowledges into the world, offering them as truths which can unite those committed to an anti-capitalist politics (Dean, 2019). In this way, the fight for subjugated knowledges represents an effort to ascend into humanity (Mbembe, 2021).

De-linking from capitalism is a task that is epistemic and rational inasmuch as it is economic and political (Amin, 1989; Ndlovu-Gatsheni, 2021). For those psychologists of community who are concerned with epistemic freedom, working with community members must entail building a new, humanist rationality that embodies a multitude of knowledges and collective knowledge-making practices. A rationality of this sort does not lay a claim to knowing the world in its totality. Instead, it represents an epistemic position whereby different ways of knowing the world (which has always been a world of worlds; see Holloway, 2010) are acknowledged (Wark, 2020), with anti-capitalist action becoming the mechanism through which to honour the truth of such epistemic pluriversality.

Love and Care

Ron Roberts (2015) argues that in resisting neoliberal capitalism and its accompanying rationality, psychologists should strive to connect psychology and politics not with obedience or fear, but more noble human possibilities like love and care. However, what might we mean by these two terms that seem so bound to the instrumental banality of neoliberal metrics? Although love and care are often grouped together or used interchangeably to denote sentimentality and/or sacrosanct duty, I have argued that the two are fundamentally different, albeit related, political (and even politicising) concepts. To begin with, and following Terry Eagleton (2004), I understand love as a radical openness to the needs of others as well as the self as it is formed intersubjectively. Love, in this regard, is not a fleeting feeling. It represents a disposition that determines how one acts, thinks, and feels (see Wittgenstein, 1967). Resultantly, love sees both affect and action working together to produce knowledges (i.e. ways of knowing the love disposition) as well as an ethic (i.e. how we ought to live in order to facilitate the conditions necessary to stand in the love disposition) (Malherbe, 2021). Care, on the other hand, is not a disposition. Care is labour. Specifically, care is the socially reproductive labour that sees to the physical and/or emotional needs of others and ourselves (Care Collective, 2020; Malherbe, 2020). Care is crucial for making, remaking, and repairing the world in which we live (Dowling, 2021) and is what reproduces those involved in the kinds of productive labour which are more readily recognised as labour. Love and care are, of course, not mutually exclusive concepts. Assuming the love disposition usually means taking on some sort of care work. However, because care is socially necessary (i.e. societies will cease being reproduced without caring labour), it is not de facto carried out from within the love disposition.

Love and care have been thoroughly subsumed by neoliberal rationality. Love, I have argued (see Malherbe, 2021), is repeatedly subject to neoliberal metrics that resemble psychopolitics (e.g. dating websites that require people to, and reward them for, marketing the self *a la* homo economicus); biopolitics (e.g. mobilising an unrelenting work ethic through the compulsion to "love what you do"); and the necropolitical logic of private property (e.g. the imperative to own and control the loved object with little-to-no regard for life beyond, or even the life of, this object). When subjected to neoliberal rationality, care work is similarly made into a commodified and alienating duty. For instance, we see how patriarchal capitalism operates through traditional morality when care is expected from women qua women. This expectation remains underpaid or unpaid and is therefore given little value within neoliberal rationality's economising perceptions of worthiness (Fraser et al., 2019; Malherbe, 2020). When the very care work that is required to sustain life and society is cheapened and unregulated in these ways, such work tends to fall on the shoulders of the most economically precarious (oftentimes female) members of a population who, in turn, are afforded few opportunities to care in their own lives (Dowling, 2021). Both love and care are limited and deformed when placed within a task-oriented neoliberal rationality, and neither is afforded the necessary support or time (see Fromm, 1962). Indeed, when shot through with neoliberal rationality, love becomes little other than the love of one's ingroup (Ahmed, 2015), and care describes little other than one's duty to serve (Federici, 1975). The relational and affective dimensions of each become debased so that their physical requirements can seem sacrosanct (Dowling, 2021). It is difficult, then, to enact care and almost impossible to stand in the love disposition when both are cheapened and/or systematically attacked (see Malherbe, 2021).

Martin Luther King Jr., Alexandra Kollontai, Paulo Freire, Frantz Fanon, Emma Goldman, Karl Marx, and Che Guevara all spoke of an anti-capitalism that would support love and also (although perhaps to a lesser extent) care between people (see Dean, 2019; hooks, 2000; York, 2021). I, too, wish to emphasise that love and care represent important inroads to challenging neoliberal rationality, with the task of an anti-capitalist psychology of community being one of working with people to unite the affective with the physical in practices of love and care, bringing forth visions and enactments of each that are de-linked from oppressive neoliberal rationality. Put differently, an anti-capitalist psychology of community is concerned with love and care insofar as each can be undertaken as collective enterprises, free from privatisation and/or the imperative to control. The struggle is, thus, to fight for a world in which it is structurally easier to stand in the love disposition and where care work is valued and socialised democratically.

An anti-capitalist psychology of community can be used to ensure that within political movements, relations between activists reflect love and care in ways that do not cohere with neoliberal rationality. Looking, firstly, at love: in what is sometimes referred to as "loving critique", psychologists of community can work with activists to facilitate organisational spaces wherein disagreements are understood as generative interactions between comrades (Bohrer, 2020). Within these spaces, both the knowledge and ethic contained within the love disposition can be articulated in ways that allow for reflexive interactions among activists who seek to deepen their commitment to an anti-capitalist politics. It is in this very precise way that the ordinariness of love can be useful for emancipatory practice (see York, 2021), rendering such practice part of rational thinking. Loving critique is, therefore, not intended to shame comrades. It is always undertaken with the express purpose of igniting the sorts of critical reflexivity discussed in Chap. 3, and as such, it is geared towards ensuring that the anti-capitalist politics with which one is engaged is, indeed, open to the needs of others with whom one struggles. At the same time, actioning the love disposition through loving critique does not denote a love that is contradiction-free. Loving critique entails grappling with the difficult feelings of loss, discomfort, and loathing that a commitment to a genuinely transformative mode of anti-capitalism demands of comrades (Dean, 2019; Wilkinson, 2017). Difficult feelings like these need not debilitate activists. They can, instead, strengthen the very internal relations upon which political movements depend by embracing the differences, antagonisms, multiplicities, and tensions that characterise these movements (Hardt, 2011; York, 2021).

Moving on, then, to care within anti-capitalist struggle: ensuring that comrades are fed, laying out and packing up the chairs at political meetings, and taking on the political duties of those who physically and/or psychologically can no longer do so all constitute examples of the kinds of socially reproductive labour which is imperative for sustaining anti-capitalist struggle and in effect represent a caring commitment to this struggle (see Dean, 2019). Yet, such care work—even though it is performed for purposes of anti-capitalism—oftentimes reflects neoliberal rationality in that it goes unacknowledged and/or is feminised in essentialising ways within movements. However, the caring society for which people are struggling should be reflected in the forms assumed by their political movements, forms which can—in turn—influence the content of a movement's political demands (Holloway, 2010). An anti-capitalist psychology of community can be used to facilitate spaces wherein comrades discuss how it is that care work can be democratised, cherished, and properly recognised within their movements. These conversations (which, for some, will undoubtedly be difficult) are essential for reconnecting the physical with the affective in care work and for conceiving of care beyond neoliberal rationality.

In considering all of the above, I wish to emphasise that an anti-capitalist psychology of community should fetishise neither love nor care (i.e. these concepts should not be invested with powers that negate the processes that went into constituting their existence; see Holloway, 2010; Mbembe, 2001). Neither love nor care should be harnessed to demand that people endure what they should not have to (e.g. gender-based violence, unsupported or undervalued domestic labour, allyship with abusive comrades; see Wilkinson, 2017). Both concepts must be troubled if they are to be used to construct new, anti-capitalist rationalities (see Malherbe, 2021). In re-joining the physical and the affective components of love and care, psychologists of community and activists should embrace each with caution and with a readiness to abandon these concepts if they are in any way being used to reproduce the kinds of oppression that neoliberal rationality has sought to make common sense.

Thomas Teo (2018) notes that "The pretence of care for the other is no longer required in an anonymous labor market (yet pretence might be required for certain service jobs)" (p. 595). However, because care—as well as love—connects the private with the public and thus transforms the self, society, and others (York, 2021), both hold considerable anti-capitalist potential. An anti-capitalist psychology of community that strives to replicate and systematise democratic, material, affective, and collective conceptions of love and care does so in the knowledge that each has been successfully embraced by neoliberal rationality. The point, then, is to "assert a different type of doing" when it comes to love and care (Holloway, 2010, p. 21), envisioning both from within the vulnerabilities of capitalism in order to expose these vulnerabilities and reveal the absurdity of a rationality that values an economic system wherein even the most basic kinds of human connection are structurally disallowed.

Case Illustration: Insurgent Rationalities

In an attempt to demonstrate how rationality can be pried from neoliberalism, I examine in this section how insurgent, anti-capitalist rationality shaped the daily lives and political activities of those living in Thembelihle, a low-income community in Johannesburg, South Africa. In particular, I consider how these community members made use of a documentary film that they produced (see Chapters 3 and 4) to engage, realise, and communicate such insurgent rationality.

If we begin by looking at how the documentary contributed to counter-hegemonic struggle in Thembelihle, then we must first consider how Thembelihle has been constructed in hegemonic discourse. Although studying the hegemonic discursive patterns which surround a community can, oftentimes, be more illuminating to community outsiders than to its residents, it is nonetheless useful for counter-hegemonic struggles to have a clearly articulated picture—backed up with data—of the dominant discursive landscape on which a community is situated. Therefore, I—along with Mohamed Seedat and Shahnaaz Suffla—examined how Thembelihle has been represented in the South African press (see Malherbe, Seedat, & Suffla, 2021). Conducting a discourse analysis on 377 newspaper reports, we found that within the media, Thembelihle—as a poor community—was unable to fully cohere with neoliberal rationality's economising social order. As such, the community's existence within this order was made to appear violent. Almost every mention of Thembelihle in the news (and thus whenever it entered into broader public consciousness) was in relation to baseless protest violence. Such "violence" could range from police officers firing rubber bullets at protesters from Thembelihle or protesters disrupting the traffic flow near to Thembelihle. These apparently violent protests were almost always described as "service delivery protests", thus confining the protesters' multifarious demands to the logic and rationality of the neoliberal State (see Duncan, 2016). Hegemonic constructions of this kind have several consequences for those living in Thembelihle. The work of Frantz Fanon (1967) tells us much about the psychic damage that is incurred when images of the self are mirrored back through the distortions of coloniality which, as we have seen, operate alongside and inform neoliberal rationality by fixing violence to the very character of colonised peoples. Materially, these discursive representations can be used to garner public support for State violence which, in the case of Thembelihle, has taken the form of police brutality and even, on occasion, intervention from the South African Army (see Ngwane, 2021; Poplak, 2015). State violence of this sort is most often directed at those in the community who, through protest, reject neoliberal rationality's economising conception of the human (see Duncan, 2016).

Trevor Ngwane explains that the Thembelihle Crisis Committee (or TCC, a "socialist-oriented" political movement organisation) has maintained its leadership and influence in the community for over 20 years by staying in touch with the popular sentiments of its residents, developing political programmes and positions in accordance with these sentiments (Ngwane, 2021, p. 144). It is, therefore, popular sentiment that informs how TCC advances its counter-hegemonic war of position. An example of this was noted in 2016 when TCC successfully campaigned for electricity. In addition to stressing that electricity should, as a human right, be made available to all residents of Thembelihle, the campaign also made use of a short digital story that TCC activists produced in collaboration with the Institute of Social and Health Sciences (ISHS). This digital story spoke back to hegemonic depictions of Thembelihle (exemplified in mainstream news coverage of the community) which acted to justify the State's less-than-human treatment of those living in the community (see Suffla et al., 2020).

Many of the same TCC activists who worked on this digital story were involved in producing the documentary film with the ISHS. However, because the filmic form is more ambitious than that of the digital story, the TCC activists who produced the documentary did not limit their war of position to a single-issue campaign. Instead, they engaged in the broader project of constructing a new humanism outside of neoliberal rationality. By depicting not only the history of TCC's anti-capitalist struggle in Thembelihle (including the victories that TCC had won and the State-directed repression that it continues to face) but also the day-to-day existence that such struggle defends, the documentary sought to represent the very humanity that was denied by hegemonic news reports which confined the human to homo economicus. The documentary's counter-hegemonic contribution was, therefore, noted in the way it captured the excess meaning (i.e. the humanity of Thembelihle) that was absent from mainstream media discourse. In so doing, the documentary sought to delegitimise hegemonic discourses surrounding Thembelihle by exposing the representational failures of these discourses. Specifically, violence as a definitional feature of Thembelihle was replaced with a nuanced, humanising, and sharply politicised representation of the community. In turn, people could identify with this new, counter-hegemonic discourse. As one audience member described it at a public screening event, the documentary "shows that we of Thembelihle, we are citizens of South Africa, we are human beings, we are here".

If, however, the documentary was to serve as a politically meaningful tool within TCC's war of position, it had to inform anti-capitalist action. Certainly, a desire for actioning the documentary's counter-hegemonic discourse was apparent at public screenings, exemplified in one audience member's passionate plea to take the documentary "to national government level so that they understand that, yes, we are living in an informal settlement, but we do have a vision of a better future and, as voting citizens, we deserve a better future". It was, therefore, important that the documentary be used to incorporate such popular sentiment into TCC's political agenda. This was seen to in several ways. As recounted in the previous two chapters, TCC used the documentary to foster solidarity with anti-capitalist groups from surrounding communities (see Chap. 3) as well as with low-waged workers (see Chap. 4). Added to this though, TCC activists, along with other residents from the community, worked with the ISHS to host a community campaign in Thembelihle. People from surrounding communities were invited into Thembelihle to celebrate the political and humanist victories for which the residents of Thembelihle had been fighting for over three decades. The purpose here was to establish a space wherein these different communities could articulate a better future for Thembelihle and, indeed, South Africa. The 3-day campaign was well-attended and concluded with a screening of the documentary. It was at this screening—attended by hundreds of people, including local politicians—that TCC activists made the case for their anti-capitalist programme. This was met with much excitement and engagement from audience members, many of whom had only ever interacted with Thembelihle through epistemologically violent news media reports. It was in these moments that

"Thembelihle" (a signifier with a predetermined signified) was used to encapsulate pluriversality and the anti-capitalist sentiments of those living in, but also beyond, the community.

Regarding the everyday, although documentary film is not an appropriate medium for capturing the "hidden scripts" (see Scott, 1985) of everyday resistance in the workplace because doing so would bring such resistance to the fore (and thus would diminish its power), documentaries can articulate the "alternative logic" (Baldacchino, 1990, p. 467) of everyday activity which can, in turn, inform the kinds of organised anti-capitalist resistance discussed in Chap. 3. The documentary depicted how, in Thembelihle, an anti-capitalist everyday was being enacted within economic activities that privileged community ownership and participation over neoliberal rationality and the profit motive. Hardt and Negri (2017) refer to such activity as entrepreneurship of the multitude, a term which speaks to a form of labour that is infused with an ethos of cooperation, social consciousness, and democratic decision-making, all of which defy neoliberalism's entrepreneurship of capital (see Harvey, 2020). Entrepreneurship of the multitude offers an excellent example of *détournement* in action, whereby the notion of entrepreneurship is pried from neoliberal rationality and remade through the logic of anti-capitalism.

Although the documentary depicted several examples of entrepreneurship of the multitude in Thembelihle, I will focus on the two cases that seemed to resonate most with audiences. The first was a brick-making worker-run cooperative. Worker cooperatives, simply put, are autonomous associations of people who, together, try to meet their economic needs through jointly owned and democratically run enterprises, instituting direct action at the micro-level with the hope of effecting larger, macro-level economic structures (Khumalo, 2014). The documentary depicted how those within the brick-making cooperative divided up labour democratically, distributed profits equally, and tied the work itself to infrastructure developments in Thembelihle (particularly, the electrification of the community for which TCC had successfully campaigned a few years earlier). The second example of entrepreneurship of the multitude depicted in the documentary concerned Thembelihle's social and solidarity economy (see Wright, 2019), whereby a small-scale farmer sells his produce (which, he insists, is always healthy and fresh) in accordance with what people are able to pay, which sometimes means giving it away free of charge. As he describes his business in the documentary: "This garden reflects the people of Thembelihle" and, therefore, could not exist in relation to the profit motive exclusively. Both of these examples, in quite different ways, sought to embed anti-capitalist rationality within everyday community activity.

In depicting Thembelihle's entrepreneurship of the multitude, the documentary demonstrated how anti-capitalism was being enacted in the here and now and how people were able to exit—albeit briefly—the capitalist mode of production. Anti-capitalism was, in this sense, rendered thinkable, liveable, community-centred, and ethical. Members of the TCC who watched the documentary connected the entrepreneurship of the multitude with their own, formalised anti-capitalist resistance. As one TCC activist proclaimed:

> We don't have to just ignore it [poverty in Thembelihle] and say "oh, it's normal". They [community members featured in the documentary] want the best from their place. That's why there's all this action ... there's this brother ... that's doing a garden [the farmer] ... he did encourage me ... everything that we do, we have to take away money, always, but ... he can spend it on his garden and a social group. As people, we have to care for each [other]. Don't say "no, I'm fine. I'm not poor. I'm not sick. I'm not hungry". You must be conscious!

Structural support for the anti-capitalist everyday is, however, essential if such activity is to be sustained. This was made clear in the very different outcomes of the farmer and the brick-making workers' cooperative. For the farmer, the documentary formed part of his successful effort to register his community garden as a non-profit organisation. This kind of institutional support, he told me, enabled him to expand his contribution to Thembelihle's social and solidarity economy. The cooperative did not, however, see as positive an outcome. As work became scarcer in Thembelihle, especially after the electrification of the community was completed, the cooperative shut down. This is, unfortunately, often the case among unsupported worker-owned enterprises in South Africa (Khumalo, 2014). Within the documentary, one of the cooperative's brick-makers seems to anticipate this very outcome when he notes that he is "not sure what will happen [to the cooperative] when the electricity project ends" and that "this is no business, it is child's play. We are just working to eat". This final sentence seems to reflect his desire to work outside of the dictates of neoliberal rationality. The task, then, for an anti-capitalist psychology of community is to create spaces that are geared towards gaining support for the anti-capitalist everyday, such as the entrepreneurship of the multitude. A robust and interconnected anti-capitalist everyday can, in turn, create greater social cohesion within communities (see Khumalo, 2014) and foster solidarity among community-led social movements and institutions (see Baldacchino, 1990).

In considering what I have said about the documentary's counter-hegemonic capacities and its depictions of the anti-capitalist everyday, we can see how it sought to honour epistemic freedom by interpreting Thembelihle from the perspectives of those who live there. It was in this sense that the documentary attempted to combat the kinds of epistemic violence exemplified in mainstream news media reporting on Thembelihle (see Malherbe, Seedat, & Suffla, 2021). In many ways, the documentary served as a repository for activist knowledges and knowledges of everyday resistance, both of which are rendered useless, damaging, and/or unreasonable when measured against neoliberal rationality. By depicting how anti-capitalism is embedded within Thembelihle, the documentary exercised a mode of epistemic freedom by connecting the common, the shared, and the emancipatory with the ordinary.

It was, however, not only the documentary's content but also its productive form that emphasised the collective, ongoing nature of knowledge-making in Thembelihle. The participatory nature of the documentary (whereby several community-based groups were involved in its conceptualisation, shooting, editing, and screening events) ensured that the knowledges it offered were, as far as possible, democratically constructed and distributed. Such collaboration was not always without tension. People often disagreed about what was being depicted in the documentary or how these depictions were approached. At the various screening events, audiences and film producers would also discuss what they understood as gaps within the documentary (see, e.g. Chap. 3). These disagreements came to represent epistemic frictions that guarded against exclusions and regulatory practices within knowledge-making, highlighting the multitudinous nature of knowing.

Epistemic freedom demands that people fight for the material conditions required to produce and sustain the subaltern knowledges that enable knowing the world (which is always a world of worlds; see Holloway, 2010) in different ways. In an attempt, then, to connect the political with the epistemic, the documentary depicted how a progressive day-care school principal in the community was fighting for the educational resources that would allow her to teach in a way that was not chained to neoliberal rationality. In the documentary, she explains that "Education is important, that's why we're trying to educate not only the kids but the parents as well … we're trying to promote and improve the learning culture within our community". She goes on to say that:

> Our biggest challenge is funds. Our school fees is the only source of income … [from which] we have … to pay the teachers, we have to provide the food for the children, we have to make sure that the resources are there, we have to make sure that the crèche is maintained. Another challenge is that because of the area that we are in, we have difficulties with the social development, where they'll be telling us that you don't qualify because of the area. When we go to the counsellor, the counsellor will tell you that Thembelihle shouldn't even be here".

Here, she connects the conditions required to foster epistemic freedom to anti-capitalist struggle, demonstrating how material struggle is bound up with struggles for epistemic freedom. As such, audiences were offered a new political vocabulary through which to interpret and connect anti-capitalist struggles. The fight for a "learning culture" was also the fight for sanitation, food, and State recognition, with each interpreted through the register of the other, thus highlighting the totalising purview that a persuasive anti-capitalist rationality must assume.

Finally, we must consider love and care in relation to this documentary project. Beginning with care, the documentary's primary depiction of caring labour centred on two nurses working in the community. On camera, each nurse described how their labours connect to the reproduction of Thembelihle's multitude (see Hardt & Negri, 2017). As one of them describes it:

> If a sick person lives alone, we bathe them and clean their environment. If there is no food, we make a plan for them … If there is a family nearby who can help, we train that family in how to look after that person. And we return to monitor that person to see how they are looking after the sick person.

Both nurses resisted how a neoliberal rationality based on traditional morality insists that socially reproductive labour is less fundamental to maintaining the economy than so-called material or industrial labour.

The two nurses also connected their care work to TCC's demands for socially just living conditions. As one recounts:

When it rains it's a problem. It gets very windy. In those conditions we have to go into the field. They will tell you: "you work in the community, so rain or no rain, you have to go to work". It would help if the government would provide transport … Patients also need transport to get to the clinic. The wheelchairs are also not up to standard and they've stopped giving us allowances to take wheelchairs into the community to help patients there … They will tell you: "you work in the community, so rain or no rain, you have to go to work".

Later, this same nurse goes on to say that "the spirit is there in Thembelihle. People want to see themselves living like people in other communities where there is everything ... They're fighting for what they want". Many care workers in the audience resonated strongly with these sentiments, sharing their own stories and struggles around reproductive labour. Those within and outside of activist groups like TCC voiced their dismay at the cheapening of such labour in the community. Following this, discussions centred on the necessity of incorporating reproductive labour struggles into TCC's anti-capitalist programme (e.g. ensuring that the State affords care workers adequate facilities, fairer wages, and decent working hours).

Care work was also seen to in the political meetings which were set up to discuss the issues raised at documentary screenings. These spaces were organised, cleaned, and dismantled collectively. Nevertheless, even though all community members were invited to these meetings, they were being attended primarily by men. Responding to this, a very committed feminist colleague suggested that people be encouraged to bring their children to the meetings. As childrearing remains the kind of caring labour that is unfairly and arbitrarily expected of women (Fraser et al., 2019), this invitation to bring children along meant that, soon enough, women outnumbered men at the meetings. Many of the men, especially the elder activists, were uncomfortable with the kinds of childrearing activities that now took place at these (formerly male-dominated) meetings (e.g. breastfeeding, diaper changing, the soothing of crying babies). However, such discomfort served as a point of necessary friction that, once again, emphasised the unacceptable neglect of caring labour within activist spaces. Physically bringing such care into these politicised spaces served to highlight its status as an anti-capitalist imperative.

Although care was salient in the documentary, love was perhaps less so. However, at screening spaces, I observed instances of love in people's receptiveness to the needs of one another, which was especially the case when people declared the need to dedicate themselves to some sort of anti-capitalist project (whether this was the organised political activities of TCC or the everyday anti-capitalism exemplified by the entrepreneurship of the multitude). There was also considerable loving critique at the various screenings, whereby disagreement was harnessed by audiences not to shame comrades, but to open up their commitment to a range of anti-capitalist struggles. Some of these moments of loving critique were discussed in Chap. 3 with regard to critical reflexivity (e.g. challenges to those, including myself, who were able to and often did exercise power disproportionately at the screening events). We can also understand the debates around childcaring at political meetings, discussed above, as moments of loving critique. Although loving critique usually instated a rather tense atmosphere that was characterised by difficult, even draining, antagonistic engagements which were rarely fruitful in any immediate sense, such critique served to prevent neoliberal rationality from structuring these anti-capitalist spaces. In this respect, loving critique was deployed in an attempt to strengthen the anti-capitalist commitments and capacities of the collective.

I have presented a range of activities and interventions here in an effort to argue that the pervasiveness of neoliberal rationality need not overwhelm or debilitate a psychology of community's attempts to assist in the establishment of anti-capitalist rationalities. Instead, we should be driven to seek out and identify the anti-capitalist rationalities which are already in circulation and offer the kinds of material and psychic support required to sustain, strengthen, and spread such rationality.

Conclusion

Resisting the ways that neoliberal rationality bends nearly everything in its purview to a constraining model of the economic is tremendously challenging. This is because such resistance is defined by a kind of action that simultaneously refuses and creates. Indeed, resisting neoliberalism's dehumanising rationality requires both a "ruthless criticism of all that exists" (Marx & Engels, 1975, p. 142) and the establishment of an insurgent, anti-capitalist rationality. This new rationality must seek to be more ambitious and more persuasive than neoliberal rationality and is, therefore, an ongoing, always adapting, and collective undertaking. I have attempted in this chapter to map out how an anti-capitalist psychology of community can assist people in resisting neoliberal rationality by making itself of use to counter-hegemonic struggles, everyday resistance, the fight for epistemic freedom, and the systematic implementation of love and care. It is through these kinds of insurgent rationality that anti-capitalism can be rendered as expansive and ambitious as it is appealing and urgent. As with my reflections on resisting the neoliberal political project (Chap. 3) and neoliberal ideology (Chap. 4), this chapter is necessarily incomplete. I would encourage others to build upon, contest, improve, and criticise what I have said here so that we can strengthen the emancipatory potentialities of an anti-capitalist psychology of community.

References

Ahmed, S. (2015). *The cultural politics of emotion*. Routledge.

Amin, S. (1989). *Eurocentrism*. Zed Books.

Amin, S. (2014). *The implosion of capitalism*. Pluto Press.

Baldacchino, G. (1990). A war of position: Ideas on a strategy for worker cooperative development. *Economic and Industrial Democracy, 11*(4), 463–482.

Bohrer, A. (2020). *Marxism and intersectionality: Race, gender, class and sexuality under contemporary capitalism*. Columbia University Press.

Brown, W. (2015). *Undoing the demos: Neoliberalism's stealth revolution*. Zone Books.

Cabral, A. (2016). *Resistance and decolonization*. Rowman & Littlefield International.

Carroll, W. K. (2009). Hegemony, counter-hegemony, anti-hegemony. *Socialist Studies/Études socialistes, 2*, 9–43.

Chibber, V. (2022). *The class matrix: Social theory after the cultural turn*. Harvard University Press.

Care Collective. (2020). *The care manifesto: The politics of interdependence*. Verso.

Collins, C. (2003). 'Critical psychology' and contemporary struggles against neoliberalism. *Annual Review of Critical Psychology, 3*, 26–48.

Cornell, J., Seedat, M., Malherbe, N., & Suffla, S. (2020). Splintered politics of memory and community resistance. *Journal of Community Psychology, 48*(5), 1677–1695.

De Cleen, B., Goyvaerts, J., Carpentier, N., Glynos, J., & Stavrakakis, Y. (2021). Moving discourse theory forward: A five-track proposal for future research. *Journal of Language and Politics, 20*(1), 22–46.

de Sousa Santos, B. (2016). *Epistemologies of the south. Justice against epistemicide*. Routledge.

Dean, J. (2019). *Comrade: An essay on political belonging*. Verso.

Debord, G. (1977). *Society of the spectacle*. Black & Red.

Dowling, E. (2021). *The care crisis: What caused it and how can we end it?* Verso.

Duncan, J. (2016). *Protest nation: The right to protest in South Africa*. University of KwaZulu-Natal Press.

Eagleton, T. (2004). *After theory*. Penguin.

Fairclough, N. (2003). *Analysing discourse: Textual analysis for social research*. Routledge.

Fanon, F. (1967). *Black skin, white masks*. Grove.

Federici, S. (1975). *Wages against housework*. Falling Wall Press.

Foucault, M. (1971). Orders of discourse. *Social Science Information, 10*(2), 7–30.

Fraser, N., Arruzza, C., & Bhattacharya, T. (2019). *Feminism for the 99 percent: A manifesto*. Verso.

Fromm, E. (1962). *The art of loving*. Harper & Row.

Gramsci, A. (1971). *Selections from the prison notebooks*. Lawrence & Wishart.

Hall, S. (1997). Introduction. In S. Hall (Ed.), *Representation: Cultural representations and signifying practices* (pp. 1–11). Sage.

Hardt, M. (2011). For love or money. *Cultural Anthropology, 26*(4), 676–682.

Hardt, M., & Negri, A. (2000). *Empire*. Harvard University Press.

Hardt, M., & Negri, A. (2009). *Commonwealth*. Harvard University Press.

Hardt, M., & Negri, A. (2017). *Assembly*. Oxford University Press.

Harrison, P. (2000). Making sense: Embodiment and the sensibilities of the everyday. *Environment and Planning D: Society and Space, 18*(4), 497–517.

Harvey, D. (2017). *Marx, capital, and the madness of economic reason*. Oxford University Press.

Harvey, D. (2020). *The anti-capitalist chronicles*. Pluto Press.

Holloway, J. (2010). *Crack capitalism*. Pluto Press.

hooks, b. (2000). *All about love: New visions*. William Morrow and Company.

Johansson, A., & Vinthagen, S. (2020). *Conceptualizing "everyday resistance": A transdisciplinary approach*. Routledge.

Khumalo, P. (2014). Improving the contribution of cooperatives as vehicles for local economic development in South Africa. *African Studies Quarterly, 14*(4), 61–79.

Laclau, E., & Mouffe, C. (1985). *Hegemony and socialist strategy: Toward a radical democratic politics*. Verso.

Lazarus, S. (2018). *Power and identity in the struggle for social justice: Reflections on community psychology practice*. Springer.

Lefebvre, H. (2002). *Critique of everyday life: Foundations for a sociology of the everyday, 2*, Verso.

Malherbe, N. (2020). Community psychology and the crisis of care. *Journal of Community Psychology, 48*(7), 2131–2137.

Malherbe, N. (2021). Considering love: Implications for critical political psychology. *New Ideas in Psychology, 61*, 100851.

Malherbe, N., Ratele, K., Adams, G., Reddy, G., & Suffla, S. (2021). A decolonial Africa(n)-centered psychology of antiracism. *Review of General Psychology, 25*(4), 437–450.

Malherbe, N., Seedat, M., & Suffla, S. (2021). Analyzing discursive constructions of community in newspaper articles. *American Journal of Community Psychology, 67*(3–4), 433–446.

Malherbe, N., Suffla, S., & Seedat, M. (2022). Epistemicide and epistemic freedom: Reflections for a decolonising community psychology. In C. Kagan, J. Akhurst, J. Alfaro, R. Lawthom, M. Richards, & A. Zambrano (Eds.), *The Routledge international handbook of community psychology: Facing global crises with hope* (pp. 17–31). Routledge.

Marx, K. (1973). *Grundrisse*. Penguin.

Marx, K., & Engels, F. (1975). In I. Vol (Ed.), *Collected works*. International Publishers.

Mbembe, A. (2001). *On the postcolony*. University of California Press.

Mbembe, A. (2019). *Necropolitics*. Wits University Press.

Mbembe, A. (2021). *Out of the dark night: Essays on decolonization*. Wits University Press.

Medina, J. (2011). Toward a Foucaultian epistemology of resistance: Counter-memory, epistemic friction, and guerrilla pluralism. *Foucault Studies, 12*, 9–35.

Montero, M., Sonn, C. C., & Burton, M. (2017). Community psychology and liberation psychology: A creative synergy for an ethical and transformative praxis. In M. A. Bond, I. Serrano-García, C. B. Keys, & M. Shinn (Eds.), *APA handbook of community psychology* (Vol. *1*, pp. 149–167). American Psychological Association.

Ndlovu-Gatsheni, S. J. (2018). The dynamics of epistemological decolonisation in the 21st century: Towards epistemic freedom. *Strategic Review for Southern Africa, 40*(1), 16–45.

Ndlovu-Gatsheni, S. J. (2021). Revisiting Marxism and decolonisation through the legacy of Samir Amin. *Review of African Political Economy, 48*(167), 50–65.

Ngwane, T. (2021). *Amakomiti: Grassroots democracy in South African shack settlements*. Pluto Press.

Poks, M. (2015). Epistemic disobedience and decolonial healing in Norma Elía Cantú's Canícula. *Studia Anglica Posnaniensia, 50*(2–3), 63–80.

Poplak, R. (2015). The army vs. Thembelihle: Where the truth lies. *Daily Maverick*. Retrieved from https://www.dailymaverick.co.za/article/2015-05-05-the-army-vsthembelihle-where-the-truth-lies/

Potter, J., & Wetherell, M. (1987). *Discourse and social psychology: Beyond attitudes and behaviour*. Sage.

Rappaport, J. (1995). Empowerment meets narrative: Listening to stories and creating settings. *American Journal of Community Psychology, 23*(5), 795–807.

Ratele, K. (2019). *The world looks like this from here: Thoughts on African psychology*. Wits University Press.

Roberts, R. (2015). *Psychology and capitalism: The manipulation of mind*. Zero Books.

Rosales, C., & Langhout, R. D. (2020). Just because we don't see it, doesn't mean it's not there: Everyday resistance in psychology. *Social and Personality Psychology Compass, 14*(1), e12508.

Rutherford, A. (2018). Feminism, psychology, and the gendering of neoliberal subjectivity: From critique to disruption. *Theory & Psychology, 28*(5), 619–644.

Saad-Filho, A. (2017). Neoliberalism. In D. Brennan, D. Kristjanson-Gural, C. Mulder, & K. Olsen (Eds.), *Routledge handbook of Marxian economics* (pp. 245–254). Routledge.

Scott, J. C. (1985). *Weapons of the weak*. Yale University Press.

Scott, J. C. (1989). *Everyday forms of resistance. Copenhagen Papers, 4*, 33–62.

Seedat, M., & Suffla, S. (2017). Community psychology and its (dis)contents, archival legacies and decolonisation. *South Africa Journal of Psychology, 47*(4), 421–431.

Smith, L. T. (2021). *Decolonizing methodologies: Research and indigenous peoples*. Zed Books.

Spivak, G. C. (1988). Can the subaltern speak? In L. Grossberg & C. Nelson (Eds.), *Marxism and the interpretation of culture* (pp. 271–313). University of Illinois Press.

Srnicek, N., & Williams, A. (2015). *Inventing the future: Postcapitalism and a world without work*. Verso.

Suffla, S., Malherbe, N., & Seedat, M. (2020). Recovering the everyday within and for decolonial peacebuilding through politico-affective space. In Y. G. Acar, S. M. Moss, & O. M. Uluğ (Eds.), *Researching peace, conflict, and power in the field: Methodological challenges and opportunities* (pp. 343–364). Springer.

Teo, T. (2018). Homo neoliberalus: From personality to forms of subjectivity. *Theory & Psychology,* *28*(5), 581–599.

Tigar, M. (2009). *Narratives of oppression. Human Rights Brief, 17*(1), 1–5.

Torfing, J. (2005). Discourse theory: Achievements, arguments and challenges. In D. Howarth & J. Torfing (Eds.), *Discourse theory in European politics: Identity, policy and governance* (pp. 1–32). Palgrave Macmillan.

Trott, C. D. (2016). Constructing alternatives: Envisioning a critical psychology of prefigurative politics. *Journal of Social and Political Psychology, 4*(1), 266–285.

Wark, M. (2017). *General intellects: Twenty-five thinkers for the twenty-first century.* Verso.

Wark, M. (2020). *Sensoria: Thinkers for the twentieth-first century.* Verso.

Wilkinson, E. (2017). On love as an (im)properly political concept. *Environment and Planning D: Society and Space, 35*(1), 57–71.

Wittgenstein, L. (1967). *Zettel.* Blackwell.

Wright, E. O. (2019). *How to be an anti-capitalist in the 21st century.* Verso.

York, M. (2021). Building a culture of revolutionary love: The politics of love in radical social transformation. In C. Mayer & E. Vanderheiden (Eds.), *International handbook of love: Transcultural and transdisciplinary perspectives* (pp. 177–193). Springer.

Zuboff, S. (2019). *The age of surveillance capitalism: The fight for a human future at the new frontier of power.* PublicAffairs Books.

Chapter 6
Hoping against History

McKenzie Wark concludes her book *Capital is Dead: Is This Something Worse?* with a call that rather playfully misappropriates the famous closing lines of the *Communist Manifesto*: "Workings of the world untie! You have a win to world!" (Wark, 2019, p. 169). Anti-capitalist activity, we might say, loses its "central anchor" (Wright, 2015, p. 2015) when it is preoccupied with untying the present without worlding the future. As Srnicek and Williams (2015) write: "The ambition here is to take the future back from capitalism" (p. 127). It is my wish that the previous three chapters on resisting capitalism are not read as *untying the workings of the world* for the sake of it. Instead, I hope that these chapters inform efforts to *world* anti-capitalism, whereby the oppressed seize control of and rewrite the very histories from which they have been systematically excluded, despite the fact that it is their labour and their bodies which have made these histories (see Ndlovu-Gatsheni, 2021). However, because life beyond capitalism is not a teleological certainty, an anti-capitalist psychology of community that is concerned with worlding a better future must also concern itself with hope.

For most people, capitalism defers the prosperous future that it promises and, in many ways, disallows hope. Wahbie Long (2021) argues that when people live in conditions of grinding poverty, the future is made to seem hopeless. Yet, when we build the conditions of anti-capitalism (conditions which typically arise most forcefully in the moments when capitalism breaks down, Holloway, 2010), hope is made to seem like a real possibility (Eagleton, 2019). It is when hope is generated between people who are committed to and who believe in an anti-capitalist project (see Long, 2021) that it can propel the anti-capitalist imaginary beyond absolute resistance and towards worlding. We could say that hope rejects the iron truth of capitalism—the enemy of hopeful possibility (Roberts, 2015)—and replaces it with the possibility of better, socially just, and equitable truths. Hoping for a better capitalism is, therefore, not good enough because it confines hope to the logic of despair. Ours must be a hope that is not concerned with whether the glass of our contemporary moment is half full or half empty, but with smashing the glass altogether (see Hardt & Negri, 2009) and building a pool from which all can drink.

Hope, when conceived as an anti-capitalist imperative, lives in future-oriented action, the "dual, self-antagonistic character of human doing" (Holloway, 2010, p. 86) that finds substance in materiality. Although hope cannot influence the natural world (hoping for sunny weather is, meteorologically, useless), it is essential for changing the social world (Wright, 2015). We do not hope in the belief that our situation will change when we confront it. Instead, we do so in the knowledge that change can only occur in moments of hopeful confrontation (Eagleton, 2019). Hope and struggle, therefore, support one another. When separated, these concepts are cast adrift (Freire, 1997). For the anti-capitalist, to hope is not to "hope in the dark" without a critical grounding in reality (Hayes, 2015, p. 25). It is to hope against history by confronting and offering an alternative to the wreckage of capitalist modernity.

Thembelihle, the community on which I focus in Chaps. 3 to 5 of this book, takes its name from the isiZulu words *ithemba* and *elihle*, which together translate into English as "place of good hope". As Trevor Ngwane explains:

> The name was given to the settlement early in its life by the first committees operating in the area, to convey the sense of hope that gripped the residents then. The place was 'baptised' after an episode of violent conflict in the area. The name thus represents a tenacious hanging on to the dream of building a new community against all odds, including internal fights and external threats. It seems that this determination to realise the dream became an important element of the Thembelihle collective identity. (Ngwane, 2021, p. 117)

Following Thembelihle, an anti-capitalist psychology of community should be used within democratic initiatives to build *good hope* from below. Hope of this sort both is produced by and animates anti-capitalist struggles, rendering these struggles appealing within and across communities. It is thus through a commitment to anti-capitalist politics that hope can be born from seemingly hopeless circumstances.

This book offers some hopeful pathways for an anti-capitalist psychology of community, but there are many others, and these omissions represent important considerations for future work. Yet, no matter which path one takes here, it is imperative that hope is held far beyond mainstream psychology's narrow confines. Long (2021) recounts that there is a long-held view in psychology that hope represents an infantile, individualist desire: a mere want of what one cannot have. Psychologists tend to "treat" hope by subjecting it to the capitalist reality principle: "maturing" or "taming" this infantile desire at the level of the individual (see Mosley et al., 2020). However, as Long (2021) notes, there is also a tradition within critical psychology that seeks to harness hope as an intersubjective, life-affirming yearning for a new beginning. It is within this tradition that psychology recognises how hope roots itself in the material and the actional (see Eagleton, 2019) and how individual hopes are, at the same time, shared hopes. Bryana French et al. (2020) insist that conceiving of hope in this way is integral to psychosocial healing because it furnishes the fight for social change with the belief that this fight will not necessarily be futile, despite overwhelming odds (see also Mosley et al., 2020). Hope of this kind drives resistance to the neoliberal project by offering a new, better project; it drives resistance to neoliberal ideology by hailing the subject through a pluriversal, non-economising conception of the human; and it renders anti-capitalist sentiment common sense and rational.

It is, of course, possible that hope fetishises the future, confidently offering up false images of a new dawn that, like capitalism, always relegates this dawn to a day that never seems to be our own (see Eagleton, 2019). Hope can generate itself through the logic of neoliberal rationality: the hope for one's upward class mobility, for example. However, even hope of this sort contains within it the seeds of something better than capitalism. As Eric Hobsbawm reflects in his book, *Revolutionaries*:

> the nature of hope is such that there is truth even in the lies of capitalism. The desire for a 'happy end', however commercially exploited, is [our] desire for the good life; our ever-deceived optimism, superior to unconditional pessimism, the belief that something can be done about it. (Hobsbawm, 1973, p. 166)

For an anti-capitalist psychology of community, the point is not to succumb to an unsustainable and ungrounded optimism, nor to resort to a hopeless pessimism, but to create spaces wherein people can identify and create moments of connection that sustain their collective commitment to an ever-developing, humanistic, and democratic vision of anti-capitalism (Hayes, 2015; Long, 2021). As John Holloway (2010) writes, "it is this trying to be human that is our revolutionary hope, the potential breakthrough of another world, another doing, another way of relating" (p. 251).

An anti-capitalist psychology of community should be used for both idealist and materialist purposes. The idealism of such a psychology lies in its ability to assist in articulating collective visions of emancipation that extend beyond readily available, reality-bound perceptions. These articulations can leave the impression that we could (and that we should) take up action. And with haste! The materialism of this kind of psychology is to be found in how it is drawn on to develop and strengthen the existing and potential currents of anti-capitalism within a given community. I hope that this book has made clear some of the possibilities and limitations of an anti-capitalist psychology of community, a psychology of urgency that grounds itself in the present conjuncture, that strives towards worlding liberation, and that— despite everything—hopes against history.

References

Eagleton, T. (2019). *Hope without optimism*. Yale University Press.

Freire, P. (1997). *Pedagogy of hope: Reliving pedagogy of the oppressed*. Continuum.

French, B. H., Lewis, J. A., Mosley, D. V., Adames, H. Y., Chavez-Dueñas, N. Y., Chen, G. A., & Neville, H. A. (2020). Toward a psychological framework of radical healing in communities of color. *The Counseling Psychologist, 48*(1), 14–46.

Hardt, M., & Negri, A. (2009). *Commonwealth*. Harvard University Press.

Hayes, G. (2015). The spectre of communism is not haunting psychology. *Annual Review of Critical Psychology, 12*, 20–26.

Hobsbawm, E. (1973). *Revolutionaries*. Abacus.

Holloway, J. (2010). *Crack capitalism*. Pluto Press.

Long, W. (2021). *Nation on the couch: Inside South Africa's mind*. Melinda Ferguson Books.

Mosley, D. V., Neville, H. A., Chavez-Dueñas, N. Y., Adames, H. Y., Lewis, J. A., & French, B. H. (2020). Radical hope in revolting times: Proposing a culturally relevant psychological framework. *Social and Personality Psychology Compass, 14*(1), e12512.

Ndlovu-Gatsheni, S. J. (2021). Revisiting Marxism and decolonisation through the legacy of Samir Amin. *Review of African Political Economy, 48*(167), 50–65.

Ngwane, T. (2021). *Amakomiti: Grassroots democracy in South African shack settlements*. Pluto Press.

Roberts, R. (2015). *Psychology and capitalism: The manipulation of mind*. Zero Books.

Srnicek, N., & Williams, A. (2015). *Inventing the future: Postcapitalism and a world without work*. Verso.

Wark, M. (2019). *Capital is dead: Is this something worse?* Verso.

Wright, E. O. (2015). *Understanding class*. Verso.

Index

Printed in Great Britain